Marc Roberty

The Eric Clapton Scrapbook

A CITADEL PRESS BOOK

Published by Carol Publishing Group

A Citadel Press Book
Published by Carol Publishing Group
Citadel Press is a registered trademark of Carol Communications, Inc.

Editorial Offices: 600 Madison Avenue, New York, N.Y. 10022
Sales & Distribution Offices: 120 Enterprise Avenue, Secaucus, N.J. 07094
In Canada: Canadian Manda Group, P.O. Box 920, Station U, Toronto, Ontario M8Z 5P9

Queries regarding rights and permissions should be addressed to Carol Publishing Group, 600 Madison Avenue, New York, N.Y. 10022

Carol Publishing Group books are available at special discounts for bulk purchases, for sales promotions, fund-raising, or educational purposes. Special editions can be created to specifications. For details contact: Special Sales Department, Carol Publishing Group, 120 Enterprise Avenue, Secaucus, N.J. 07094

A special thanks goes to Virginia Lohle of Starfile, for all her help with this edition.

Manufactured in the United States of America
10 9 8 7 6 5 4 3 2 1

Library of Congress Cataloging-in-Publication Data

Roberty, Marc.
    The Eric Clapton scrapbook / Mark Roberty.
        p.   cm.
    "A Citadel Press book."
    ISBN 0-8065-1454-X
    1. Clapton, Eric.   2. Rock musicians—England—Biography.
I. Title.
ML419.C58R62   1993
787.87'166'092—dc20
    [B]   93-42787
                                                      CIP
                                                      MN

INTRODUCTION

Eric Patrick Clapton was born on March 30, 1945, at the home of his grandparents, Rose and Jack Clapp, a modest terraced house on The Green in Ripley, Surrey. He was the illegitimate son of Patricia Molly Clapton, who was unmarried, and Edward Fryer, a Canadian soldier stationed in England. After the war Edward Fryer returned to a wife in Canada and thus dropped out of Eric's life forever. Pat Clapton later married a Canadian soldier named Frank McDonald and moved to Germany and then to Canada. Young Eric was raised by his grandparents in Ripley, an area of the English Home Counties for which he has retained an abiding affection. To this day he lives within a short drive of his birthplace.

From age five, Eric attended Ripley Church of England Primary School. At first he appeared to be a bright child, well capable of passing the then all important eleven-plus examination and going on to grammar school, but this proved not to be the case and instead he went to St. Bede's Secondary Modern at Send, near Woking. Here he showed a natural talent for art and at fourteen he was transferred to Hollyfield Road School, Surbiton, which housed the junior department of Kingston College of Art. Two years later he moved on to Kingston Art College proper to study graphic design.

In the meantime Eric had discovered the guitar. His first guitar, a thirteenth birthday present from Rose and Jack Clapp, was a £14 acoustic from Bell's music shop in Kingston, and before long almost all his waking hours were spent mastering the instrument. It accompanied him on the daily bus journey to Kingston and was the principal reason why he was

asked to leave Art School at sixteen. His first paid employment was as a casual laborer and as a temporary postman over Christmas 1961.

Eric's earliest musical leanings developed into areas more demanding than the current pop music of the day. He became interested in authentic American blues and listened in admiration to records by such American black performers as Big Bill Broonzy, Muddy Waters, Howlin' Wolf, and, most crucially, Robert Johnson, the legendary bluesman from Mississippi who was said to have sold his soul to the devil in exchange for a musical virtuosity that inspired awe-struck envy in his peers. Johnson's mysterious early death, allegedly at the hands of a jealous husband, added credence and fascination to the legend.

Such colorful tales of errant bluesmen from the past might likely have entranced young Eric as he struggled to emulate the tormented emotional performances of these American mentors on his second guitar, a £100 Kay electric. Thus equipped, he joined his first band, The Roosters, after an invitation from their guitarist, Tom McGuinness, whose girlfriend attended Kingston Art College and who had observed Eric practicing during lunch breaks. In addition to McGuinness and Clapton, The Roosters included Ben Palmer (piano), Terry Brennan (vocals), and Robin Mason (drums). When Eric joined, McGuinness switched to bass.

The Roosters stayed together for the first six months of 1963, operating around the Richmond area playing rhythm and blues numbers like "Hoochie Coochie Man" and "Boom Boom." Unlike Eric, most of their members had day jobs and to them the band was a

secondary occupation. They played a couple of opening shows at the Marquee Club in London but disbanded through a mixture of apathy and lack of outside encouragement.

Eric and Tom McGuinness then briefly joined The Engineers, a band put together to back Casey Jones, one-time leader of a Liverpool band called The Casanovas which had since deserted its singer and rechristened itself The Big Three. The gig lasted a month.

Eric Clapton's next band was to bring him to the attention of a far wider public. He met them at the Crown pub in Kingston, Surrey, and was invited to enlist after making a disparaging remark about their guitarist, Paul Samwell-Smith. Their name was The Yardbirds.

1963

SEPTEMBER 1963

Eric rehearses with The Yardbirds at the Great Western pub in Richmond, Surrey. Members of the band are impressed and hire him on the spot. It would not be too unfair to say that Eric was superior to the others as a musician and certainly more in tune with the latest fashions. Both these assets were later to help the group secure television appearances.

That is not to say the others were not adept, because they were quick learners and were to make up one of the most influential bands of the sixties, even if they are only remembered for their lead guitarists.

The band comprises, at this time, Jim McCarty on drums, Chris Dreja on guitar and vocals, Paul Samwell-Smith on bass, Keith Relf on vocals and harmonica, and, of course, Eric on lead guitar and occasional vocals.

They tour the local R & B club circuit and later venture out to other parts of England.

The set list is taken from the following: "Boom Boom," "Louise," "Smokestack Lightning," "Honey in Your Hips," "Baby What's Wrong," "Carol," "I Wish You Would," "Let It Rock," "You Can't Judge a Book by the Cover," "Who Do You Love," "Little Queenie," "I'm a Man."

20, 27, 29
Studio 51, Leicester Square, London

OCTOBER 1963
4, 6, 13
Studio 51, Leicester Square, London

20
Studio 51, Leicester Square, London (2 shows 4:00 and 6:30)
Crawdaddy Club, Richmond, Surrey (7:45pm)

27
Crawdaddy Club, Richmond, Surrey (7:45pm)

NOVEMBER 1963
2
Star Club, Croydon, Surrey

3
Crawdaddy Club, Richmond, Surrey

8
Edwina's Club, Finsbury Park, London

9
Star Club, Croydon, Surrey

10
Crawdaddy Club, Richmond, Surrey

15
Edwina's Club, Finsbury Park, London

16
Star Club, Croydon, Surrey

17
Crawdaddy Club, Richmond, Surrey

20
Ricky Tick, Windsor, Berkshire

22
Edwina's Club, Finsbury Park, London

23
Star Club, Croydon, Surrey

24
Crawdaddy Club, Richmond, Surrey

Right: The Yardbirds, 1964. Left to right: Paul Samwell Smith, Keith Relf, Jim McCarty, Eric Clapton, Chris Dreja. (Dezo Hoffman)

Opposite page: Eric's first appearance on vinyl. The Yardbirds pose to promote their debut single "I Wish You Would", released July 1964.

1963/ 1964

Above, right: The Yardbirds pose beside The Serpentine in Hyde Park, London. Left to right: Keith Relf, Paul Samwell Smith, Chris Dreja, Eric Clapton, Jim McCarty. (Dezo Hoffman)

29
Edwina's Club, Finsbury Park, London

30
Star Club, Croydon, Surrey

DECEMBER 1963

1
Crawdaddy Club, Richmond, Surrey

6
Edwina's Club, Finsbury Park, London

7
Star Club, Croydon, Surrey

8
Crawdaddy Club, Richmond, Surrey (Live recording of the "Sonny Boy Williamson and The Yardbirds" album.) The Yardbirds' set was also recorded and released in 1984 on the excellent "Shapes of Things" box set which is also out on CD.

Eric Clapton: **We didn't know how to back him up. It was frightening, really, because this man was real and we weren't. He wasn't very tolerant, either. I had to almost relearn how to play. It taught me a lot; it taught me the value of that music.**

13
Edwina's Club, Finsbury Park, London

14
Star Club, Croydon, Surrey

15
Civic Hall, Guildford, Surrey

17
Ricky Tick, Windsor, Berkshire

20
Plaza Ballroom, Guildford, Surrey

21, 22
Star Club, Croydon, Surrey

23
Olympia Ballroom, Reading, Berkshire

24
Ricky Tick, Windsor, Berkshire

28
Star Club, Croydon, Surrey

29
Crawdaddy Club, Richmond, Surrey

JANUARY 1964

3
Marquee Club, London

4
Star Club, Croydon, Surrey

5
Crawdaddy Club, Richmond, Surrey

10
Marquee Club, London

11
Star Club, Croydon, Surrey

12

Crawdaddy Club, Richmond, Surrey

14

Ricky Tick, Windsor, Berkshire

17

Plaza Ballroom, Guildford, Surrey

18

Star Club, Croydon, Surrey

19

Crawdaddy Club, Richmond, Surrey

20

Toby Jug Hotel, Tolworth, Surrey

21

Ricky Tick, Windsor, Berkshire

23, 24

Marquee Club, London

25

Star Club, Croydon, Surrey

Left : More shots in Hyde Park. (Pictorial Press)

Below, left: The Yardbirds performing "For Your Love," their last single on which Eric appeared, before the television cameras. Left to right: Paul Samwell Smith, Keith Relf, Chris Dreja, Eric Clapton, and Jim McCarty. (SKR Photos/LFI)

FIVE LIVE YARDBIRDS

UK Columbia SX 1677
No US release
Released January 1965

Side One:
1. Too Much Monkey Business
2. I Got Love If You Want It
3. Smokestack Lightnin'
4. Good Morning Little Schoolgirl
5. Respectable

Side Two:
6. Five Long Years
7. Pretty Girl
8. Louise
9. I'm a Man
10. Here 'Tis

1964

26

Crawdaddy Club, Richmond, Surrey

27

Toby Jug Hotel, Tolworth, Surrey

28

The Flamingo, London

30

Marquee Club, London

31

St John's Ambulance Hall, Reading, Berkshire

FEBRUARY 1964

The Yardbirds' first studio sessions take place at R. G. Jones Studios in early February during the day, while they were still touring the club circuit in the evenings. Tracks recorded are "Boom Boom," "Honey in Your Hips," "Baby What's Wrong," "I'm Talking About You," "I Wish You Would," "A Certain Girl," "You Can't Judge a Book by the Cover." These numbers are part of their live set at this time. These rough demos are taken around to Decca and EMI records by Giorgio Gomelsky, their manager. By the end of the month they had signed with EMI.

1

Pearce Hall, Maidenhead, Berkshire

2

Crawdaddy Club, Richmond, Surrey

4

Plaza Ballroom, Guildford, Surrey

6

Marquee Club, London

8

Pearce Hall, Maidenhead, Berkshire

9

Crawdaddy Club, Richmond, Surrey

11

Coronation Hall, Kingston, Surrey

13

Marquee Club, London

15

Star Club, Croydon, Surrey

16

Crawdaddy Club, Richmond, Surrey

18

Plaza Ballroom, Guildford, Surrey

20

Marquee Club, London

22

Pearce Hall, Maidenhead, Berkshire

23

Crawdaddy Club, Richmond, Surrey

25

Coronation Hall, Kingston, Surrey

27

Marquee Club, London

28

Town Hall, Birmingham, Midlands (First Rhythm and Blues Festival). All of the concert is recorded by Giorgio Gomelsky on his faithful two-track reel-to-reel. Part of the show was eventually released on an obscure French label in the seventies as "Rock Generation Series Vol. V." Catalog no. BYG 522705.

The Yardbirds' set at this time is taken from the following: "Too Much Monkey Business," "Got Love If You Want It," "Smokestack Lightning," "Good Morning Little Schoolgirl," "Respectable," "Five Long Years," "Pretty Girl," "Louise," "I'm a Man," "Here Tis," "I Wish You Would," "Little Queenie," "Carol," "Boom Boom," "I Ain't Got You."

MARCH 1964

The Yardbirds had built a strong and loyal following, so it seemed a natural idea to record one of their March shows at the Marquee for release as *Five Live Yardbirds*. However, EMI wanted a hit single first before venturing into the album market.

1

Crawdaddy Club, Richmond, Surrey

3

Coronation Hall, Kingston, Surrey

5

Marquee Club, London

6

Telephone House, Wimbledon, London

7

Pearce Hall, Maidenhead, Surrey

8

Crawdaddy Club, Richmond, Surrey

13

Marquee Club, London

15

Crawdaddy Club, Richmond, Surrey

20

Marquee Club, London

22

Crawdaddy Club, Richmond, Surrey

27

Marquee Club, London

28

Star Club, Croydon, London

29

Crawdaddy Club, Richmond, Surrey

APRIL 1964

The Yardbirds have their first real studio session at Olympic Studios in Barnes, London, for their debut single: "I Wish You Would"/"A Certain Girl."

3
Marquee Club, London

4
St. Peters Hall, Kingston, Surrey

5
Crawdaddy Club, Richmond, Surrey

7
The Refectory, Golders Green, London

10
Marquee Club, London

11
Star Club, Croydon, Surrey

12
Crawdaddy Club, Richmond, Surrey

17
Marquee Club, London

18
Star Club, Croydon, Surrey

19
Crawdaddy Club, Richmond, Surrey

21
Star Club, Croydon, Surrey

24
Marquee Club, London

25
Town Hall Ballroom, Abergavenny, Wales

26
Crawdaddy Club, Richmond, Surrey

27
The Manor House, Harringay, Essex

28
Star Club, Croydon, Surrey

MAY 1964

1
Marquee Club, London

3
Crawdaddy Club, Richmond, Surrey

4
Decca Studios, West Hampstead, London.
   Eric plays his first studio session as a guest musician on two tracks for Otis Spann. "Pretty Girls Everywhere" and "Stirs Me Up" also feature Muddy Waters on guitar, Ransome Knowling on bass, Willie Smith on drums, and Otis on vocals and piano.

Eric Clapton: **Muddy was playing rhythm guitar and I played lead, which was strange, and it was two sides we did with Mike Vernon. It was great!**

8
Marquee Club, London

10
Crawdaddy Club, Richmond, Surrey

13
Bromel Club, Bromley Court Hotel, Bromley, Kent

15
Marquee Club, London

17
Crawdaddy Club, Richmond, Surrey

22
Ready Steady Go television appearance performing "I Wish You Would." They also play at the Marquee Club, London

24
Crawdaddy Club, Richmond, Surrey

27
Beckenham Ballroom, Beckenham, Kent

29
Marquee Club, London

31
Crawdaddy Club, Richmond, Surrey

JUNE 1964

5
Marquee Club, London

7
Crawdaddy Club, Richmond, Surrey

11
Brighton Dome, Brighton, Sussex

12
Marquee Club, London

13
Club Noriek, London (all-nighter)

14
Wimbledon Palais, Wimbledon, London

19
Marquee Club, London

20
Jazz Festival, Southall, Middlesex

21
Crawdaddy Club, Richmond, Surrey

26
Northern Jazz Festival, Redcar, Cleveland

28
Crawdaddy Club, Richmond, Surrey

JULY 1964

3
Marquee Club, London

5
The Cavern, Liverpool

10, 17
Marquee Club, London

18
Second Scottish Jazz and Blues Festival, Ayr, Scotland
   After this show, The Yardbirds headed off to

1964/ 1965

Switzerland for a working holiday in Giorgio's local village.

19–23
Lugano hotel, Switzerland

Chris Dreja: **We were working virtually seven nights a week by this time, and Giorgio turned up one day and said, "We'll all take a holiday, baby, go to my village in Switzerland. There is zis club there, baby, and you can relax in the day, and we'll take some fans with us." So he organized it.**

Keith Relf had a collapsed lung due to his chronic asthma. Therefore on the band's return, Mick O'Neill from the Authentics held down the vocals with The Yardbirds for several dates until Keith was well enough to resume his role of lead singer.

24
Marquee Club, London

26
Crawdaddy Club, Richmond, Surrey

29
Bromel Club, Bromley Court Hotel, Bromley, Kent

31
Marquee Club, London

AUGUST 1964

2
Crawdaddy Club, Richmond, Surrey

4
Kenton, Middlesex (venue unknown)

7
Marquee Club, London

9
Fourth Jazz and Blues Festival, Richmond, Surrey (Mick O'Neill on vocals still, and at the end of the set they are joined by Georgie Fame, Ginger Baker, and Graham Bond for a jam session)

10
Olympic Studios, Barnes, London. The Yardbirds start recording their second single. At Eric's request, they record "Good Morning Little Schoolgirl." Keith Relf is unable to attend the session due to his continuing poor health which had started back in Lugano. His vocals will be added at a later date. They all take a well deserved holiday before resuming a hectic schedule of club dates and the dreaded package tours.

SEPTEMBER 1964

They record "I Ain't Got You" in early September, again at Olympic Studios in Barnes. This is the B side of their next single, "Good Morning Little Schoolgirl."

4
Marquee Club, London

6
Crawdaddy Club, Richmond, Surrey

11
Marquee Club, London

13
Crawdaddy Club, Richmond, Surrey
   Giorgio secures a package tour for The Yardbirds which also features Billy J. Kramer and the Nashville Teens.

18
Granada Theatre, Walthamstow

19
Colston Hall, Bristol

20
Odeon Theatre, Lewisham

21
Granada Theatre, Maidstone

22
Granada Theatre, Greenford

23
Gaumont Theatre, Ipswich

24
Odeon Theatre, Southend

25
ABC Theatre, Northampton

26
Granada Theatre, Mansfield

27
Empire Theatre, Liverpool

28
Caird Hall, Dundee

29
ABC Theatre, Edinburgh

30
Odeon Theatre, Glasgow

OCTOBER 1964

1
ABC Theatre, Dublin

2
Adelphi Theatre, Belfast

3
Savoy Theatre, Cork

4
ABC Theatre, Stockton

7
ABC Theatre, Carlisle

8
Odeon Theatre, Bolton

9
Granada Theatre, Grantham

10
ABC Theatre, Hull

11
Granada Theatre, East Ham London

13
Granada Theatre, Bedford

14
Granada Theatre, Brixton

15
Odeon Theatre, Guildford

16
ABC Theatre, Southampton

17

ABC Theatre, Gloucester

18

Granada Theatre, Tooting
   Last date of package tour before resuming club circuit.

23

Marquee Club, London

25

Crawdaddy Club, Richmond, Surrey

26

Glenlyn Club, Forest Hill, London

30

Marquee Club, London

NOVEMBER 1964

The Yardbirds record three takes of "Got to Hurry" and "Putty in Her Hands" at Olympic Studios in Barnes for possible release. They also record "Sweet Music" at IBC Studios in London, featuring Manfred Mann's Paul Jones on backing vocals. This is the first step in a deliberate move toward a more commercial sound. Eric is none too happy at this prospect as he still views himself as a blues purist.

1

Crawdaddy Club, Richmond, Surrey

6

Hippodrome, Brighton, Sussex (with Jerry Lee Lewis and Twinkle)

8

Crawdaddy Club, Richmond, Surrey
   The remainder of the month and early December is spent on another package tour.

DECEMBER 1964

Eric plays on his last session with The Yardbirds for the recording of the band's next single, "For Your Love." It is recorded at IBC Studios in London at the end of December. Written by Graham Gouldman, it was just too commercial for Eric and really had no room for him to feature his guitar. In fact he only appears on the bridge of the song. Brian Auger plays harpsichord on the session.

7

Royal Albert Hall, London (I wonder if Eric knew that one day he would be taking up a yearly residence at this venue!)

10

Olympia Ballroom, Reading, Berkshire

12

Palais, Peterborough

13

Sheffield (venue unknown)

14

Grand Pavilion, Porthcawl, Wales

17

Lakeside Ballroom, Hendon, Middlesex

18

Gravesend, Kent (venue unknown)

21

Fairfield Hall, Croydon, Surrey
   The Yardbirds are on the bill for "The Beatles' Christmas Show" which is taking place at London's Hammersmith Odeon Cinema. Other acts include Freddie and the Dreamers, Jimmy Saville, Sounds Incorporated, Elkie Brooks. They play twenty concerts with thirty-eight performances in total!
   As there are no shows on Sundays, The Yardbirds play their regular evenings at the Crawdaddy in Richmond.

24

Odeon Cinema, Hammersmith, London (1 show 7:30pm)

26

Odeon Cinema, Hammersmith, London (2 shows 6:15 and 8:45)

27

Crawdaddy Club, Richmond, Surrey

28, 29, 30, 31

Odeon Cinema, Hammersmith, London (2 shows 6:15 and 8:45)
   (Only 6:15 show on 29)

JANUARY 1965
1, 2

Odeon Cinema, Hammersmith, London (2 shows 6:15 and 8:45)

3

Crawdaddy Club, Richmond, Surrey

4, 5, 6, 7, 8, 9

Odeon Cinema, Hammersmith, London (2 shows 6:15 and 8:45)

10

Crawdaddy Club, Richmond, Surrey

11, 12, 13, 14, 15, 16

Odeon Cinema, Hammersmith, London (2 shows 6:15 and 8:45)

17

Crawdaddy Club, Richmond, Surrey

20

Bromel Club, Bromley Court Hotel, Bromley, Kent

22

Marquee Club, London

FEBRUARY 1965

The Yardbirds release their first album titled *Five Live Yardbirds*.

1, 15

Marquee Club, London

25

Eric attends Buddy Guy's London debut at the Marquee

1965

in London. Buddy, even in 1965, was doing things with a guitar that people still dream of today. To Eric, it was a revelation seeing and hearing one of his heroes.

28
Crawdaddy Club, Richmond, Surrey

MARCH 1965
1
Marquee Club, London

8
Marquee Club, London
This was probably Eric's last show with The Yardbirds, although any definite documentation is hard to find.

Eric Clapton: **My attitude within the group got really sour, and it was hinted that it would be better for me to leave. 'Cause they'd already been to see Jeff Beck play, and at the time he was far more adaptable than I was. I was withdrawing into myself, becoming intolerable, really dogmatic. So they kind of asked me to leave, and I left and felt a lot better for it.**

Keith Relf: **He loves the blues so much I suppose he didn't like it being played badly by a white shower like us.**

Eric wisely decides to take a break and gather his thoughts. He spends some time with his old friend Ben Palmer with whom he had played in the Roosters. He receives a phone call there from John Mayall asking him if he'd like to audition for The Bluesbreakers. In fact, John had once jammed with Eric when The Yardbirds were playing a show in his home town of Manchester.

John Mayall: **I'd seen Eric playing before our paths crossed and when I heard that B side of "For Your Love," it confirmed my belief in his abilities.**

The B side was "Got to Hurry," a unique piece of Eric's early greatness as a blues soloist which was later to blossom during his time with John Mayall's Bluesbreakers.

APRIL 1965
Eric joins John Mayall's Bluesbreakers which comprises John Mayall (organ, guitar, and vocals), Hughie Flint (drums), John McVie (bass). Eric is now using a Fender Telecaster before switching over to a Gibson Les Paul. In John Mayall he found someone he could relate to, and who also happened to have the best blues record collection in England. Eric plays in the style of Otis Rush and Freddie King and was delighted to find many of their singles in John's collection.

The Bluesbreakers not only tour the usual club circuit in and around London, but also travel all over Britain in a transit van.

24
BBC Studios, London
First recording with Eric. They play "Crawling Up a Hill," "Crocodile Walk," and "Bye Bye Bird."

28
Flamingo Club, Soho, London

Right: John Mayall demonstrates percussive techniques to a group of young admirers. (Dezo Hoffman)

MAY 1965
12

Levy's Recording Studio, Bond Street, London. Eric along with John Mayall, John McVie, and Hughie Flint join Bob Dylan for some informal jamming.

Tom McGuinness: **By all accounts Dylan was not on this planet when he arrived to do the recording. He played piano, with Hughie Flint on drums and Eric Clapton on guitar. The band relentlessly played "If You Gotta Go, Go Now" as a twelve-bar blues but it collapsed after forty-five seconds in complete disarray, and on the tape you hear Dylan say: "Did you get that?" There's a pause and you hear Hughie Flint say: "You've not worked much with bands, have yer, Bob?"**

15, 21, 22

Flamingo Club, Soho, London (On 15, an all-nighter)

25

Klooks Kleek, Hampstead, London

JUNE 1965

Eric records informally with Jimmy Page. The tracks were not intended for commercial use, but when both these artists became famous, the tracks appeared on *Blues Anytime* on the Immediate label.

Eric and John Mayall record two numbers for a limited edition single. Mike Vernon produced "Lonely Years" and "Bernard Jenkins" for his own label, Purdah, shortly to become Blue Horizon.

3

Cellar Club, Kingston, Surrey

4, 5, 6

Flamingo Club, Soho, London

10

Klooks Kleek, Hampstead, London

18

Pontiac Club, Zeeta House, Putney, London

19

Uxbridge Blues and Folk Festival, Uxbridge, Middlesex

JULY 1965
7

Bromel Club, Bromley Court Hotel, Bromley, Kent

8

Klooks Kleek, Hampstead, London

9, 10

Flamingo Club, Soho, London

15

College of Fashion, London

16

Ricky Tick, Windsor, Berkshire (8:00pm)

16

Flamingo Club, Soho, London (all-nighter)

24

Pontiac Club, Zeeta House, Putney, London

29

Klooks Kleek, Hampstead, London

30

Bluesville Club, Harringay

AUGUST 1965
4, 11, 25

Pontiac Club, Zeeta House, Putney, London

Eric was happy playing in The Bluesbreakers, but the

1966

BLUESBREAKERS WITH ERIC CLAPTON

UK Decca SKL4804
US London PS 492
Released July 1966

Side One:
1. All Your Love
2. Hideaway
3. Little Girl
4. Another Man
5. Double Crossing
6. What'd I Say

Side Two:
7. Key To Love
8. Parchment Farm
9. Have You Heard
10. Ramblin' on My Mind
11. Steppin' Out
12. It's All Right

constant pressure of touring and traveling in uncomfortable circumstances (sleeping in the back of a cold van) takes its toll on him. He decides to have some fun and take off into the sunset with some friends. Such is his popularity that John Mayall promises to keep Eric's place in the group open should he wish to return. Eric is living with Ben Palmer and a few other friends from Oxford and they all decide to form The Glands and tour the world! They comprise Ben Palmer (piano), John Bailey (vocals), Bob Ray (bass), Jake Milton (drums), and Bernie Greenwood (sax).

This wild idea came about after several bottles of wine, no doubt. However, they pool all their money, buy a station wagon, and drive to Greece. Of course nobody had ever heard of them and they soon realized that a support slot to a local band in an Athens restaurant was the best they could expect. The fact that they were English and that The Beatles were riding high in the charts made little to no difference.

The local Greek band are involved in a serious road accident resulting in some fatalities. The club owner had spotted Eric's potential and suddenly promoted him to playing guitar in both the support band as well as the surviving headliners!

The remaining English band members were fired a little later, leaving poor old Eric to fend for himself. The manager of the club was holding onto Eric's prized Gibson Les Paul and amplifier as leverage in case he decided to make a run for it. Luckily, Ben Palmer and Eric concocted a story for the club owner which seemed plausible. Eric told him he needed to take his guitar to get it restrung or he would be unable to play; he would, of course, leave his amplifier as guarantee. He accepted. Needless to say Eric was never to be seen again!

Eric had left two and a half months ago and now returned to England. The first thing he does is to call John Mayall, who keeps his promise and hires him back. His temporary replacement, Peter Green, was none too pleased.

NOVEMBER 1965
11
Pontiac Club, Zeeta House, Putney, London

12
Bluesville, Manor House, London

28
Flamingo Club, Soho, London

DECEMBER 1965
23
Refectory, Golders Green, London

26
Flamingo Club, Soho, London

28
Bluesville, Harringay, London

31
Bluesville, Manor House, London

JANUARY 1966
1
Flamingo Club, Soho, London

Right: Cream follows in the footsteps of The Yardbirds by having their photograph taken in Hyde Park. Left to right: Eric Clapton, Ginger Baker, Jack Bruce. (David Redfern)

Left, above and below: Eric in 1966. (Dezo Hoffman)

16
Bromel Club, Bromley Court Hotel, Bromley, Kent

17
Star Club, Croydon, Surrey

FEBRUARY 1966

Eric and John Mayall are invited to play on a session by Champion Jack Dupree. Mike Vernon is producing. The three numbers recorded with Eric are "Third Degree," "Shim-Sham-Shimmy," and "Calcutta Blues."

5
Polytechnic of Central London

6
Woolwich R&B Club, Shakespeare Hotel, London

8
Klooks Kleek, Hampstead, London

12
Polytechnic of Central London

1966

FRESH CREAM

UK Reaction 593001
US Atco SD 33-206
Released December 1966

Side One:
1. NSU
2. Sleepy Time
3. Dreaming
4. Sweet Wine
5. Spoonful
Side Two:
6. Cat's Squirrel
7. Four Until Late
8. Rollin' and Tumblin'
9. I'm So Glad
10. Toad

15
Fishmongers Arms, Woodgreen

18
Bluesville, Manor House, London

19
Flamingo Club, Soho, London

27
Bromel Club, Bromley Court Hotel, Bromley, Kent

APRIL 1966

John Mayall's Bluesbreakers enter Decca's West Hampstead Studios to record what is to be one of Eric's finest guitar playing moments on vinyl. He insists on playing at stage volume levels which present all sorts of complications for engineer Gus Dudgeon. When the album was released in August 1966, it was considered the masterpiece of the British Blues scene and it is still a firm favorite among fans.

Melody Maker: **No British musicians have ever sounded like this on record. It is a giant step. It's a credit to John and his musicians.**

Beat Instrumental: **It's Eric Clapton who steals the limelight and no doubt several copies of the album will be sold on the strength of his name.**

It is interesting to note that when the album did come out, it mentioned Eric's name on the front cover: *John Mayall's Bluesbreakers With Eric Clapton.* This was the only time that Mayall shared billing on an album cover.

6
Bluesville, Manor House, London

11
Marquee Club, Soho, London

22
Refectory, Golders Green, London

24
Bromel Club, Bromley Court Hotel, Bromley, Kent

27
Castle Club, Tooting Broadway, London

30
Flamingo Club, Soho, London

MARCH 1966

Jack Bruce was temporarily on bass as John McVie had been sacked for drinking.

Jack Bruce: **There was a great thing between me and Eric even then. He knew of me before. He'd seen me with Graham Bond a couple of times and he dug my playing.**

Eric Clapton: **There was something creative there. Most of what we were doing with Mayall was imitating the records we got, but Jack had something else — he had no** reverence for what we were doing, and so he was composing new parts as he went along playing.

Eric and Jack also take part in a one-off studio session calling themselves The Powerhouse, comprising Eric (guitar), Jack (bass), Paul Jones (harmonica), Pete York (drums), Ben Palmer (piano), Stevie Winwood (vocals and keyboards). The session takes place under the guidance of Joe Boyd for Elektra records. Three numbers are recorded, "I Want to Know," "Crossroads," "Steppin' Out."

Eric Clapton: **What happened was that guy from Elektra, Jac Holtzman, came over to England with this idea he had for an LP for recording all the international blues bands, you know, in America and in England and maybe elsewhere. He wanted a blues band that was typically representative of**

the English scene. It was kind of a toss-up between John Mayall and Spencer Davis group, I think. Then Paul Jones got in ahead of everybody and formed a scratch band which Jack Bruce and I were in; Stevie Winwood sang, Paul Jones played harp, Ben Palmer on piano."

4
Flamingo Club, Soho, London

17
Flamingo Club, Soho, London (live recording on John Mayall's two-track reel-to-reel positioned on stage)

Above left: Performing with Cream, 1966. (Nigel Dickson)

Below left: With Jack Bruce, on the set of Ready Steady Go! (Dezo Hoffman)

1966

Top left: (Jan Persson)

Others: Selecting threads with Ginger and Jack. (Pictorial Press)

18

Ram Jam Club, Brixton, London

18

Flamingo Club, Soho, London (all-nighter)

19

BBC Studios, London
Live session for radio broadcast. Numbers played are "Little Girl," "Hideaway," "Steppin' Out," "On Top of the World," "Key to Love."

20

Eel Pie Island, Twickenham, Middlesex

26

Flamingo Club, Soho, London

MAY 1966

Eric Clapton: I don't think there will be room for me here much longer. None of my music is English; it is rooted in Chicago. I represent what is going on in Chicago at the moment, the best I can anyway, because it's difficult to get all the records imported. . . . Anyway I think the only way to go is America.

It is clear that Eric is dissatisfied with just copying blues riffs and wants to progress into improvisation. He sees this as a possibility with Jack Bruce in mind.
   The Graham Bond Organisation had been playing the same circuit as The Bluesbreakers and featured Ginger Baker on drums. Ginger, in fact, had jammed with Eric on several occasions and felt he was ready for a move. So both he and Eric rehearse secretly with Jack Bruce on bass with the idea of forming a trio, despite the fact that Jack and Ginger are mortal enemies. This had come about when Jack was in the Graham Bond Organisation and both he and Ginger would argue and fight at regular intervals, both on and off stage.

Jack left and joined Manfred Mann. However, the music this new trio produced was worthwhile enough to bury the hatchet, even if it was in each other's head!

7

Ram Jam Club, Brixton, London

9

Klooks Kleek, West Hampstead, London

10

Star Hotel, Croydon, Surrey

14

Toft's Club, Folkestone, Kent

17

Fishmongers Arms, Woodgreen

21

Ricky Tick, Windsor, Berkshire

22

Flamingo Club, Soho, London

27

Refectory, Golders Green, London

30

Marquee Club, Soho, London

JUNE 1966
3

Flamingo Club, Soho, London

5

Bromel Club, Bromley Court Hotel, Bromley, Kent

10

Ram Jam Club, Brixton, London

16

Marquee Club, Soho, London

23

Fishmongers Arms, Woodgreen

25

Flamingo Club, Soho, London

Melody Maker: Groups' group starring Eric Clapton, Jack

Bruce and Ginger Baker is being formed. . . . The group say they hope to start playing clubs, ballrooms and theatres in a month's time.

Robert Stigwood: They will be called Cream and will be represented by me for agency and management. They will record for my Reaction label and go into the studios next week to cut tracks for their first single. Their debut will be at the National Jazz and Blues Festival at Windsor in July, when their single will be released.

JULY 1966

John Mayall's *Bluesbreakers With Eric Clapton* released.
   Cream enters Chalk Farm Studios to record its first single "Wrapping Paper" and "Cat's Squirrel."
   Cream's debut is in Manchester.

29

Twisted Wheel, Manchester

31

Sixth National Jazz and Blues Festival, Windsor, Berkshire

AUGUST 1966

Recording at Mayfair Sound Studios for their debut album.

2

Klooks Kleek, West Hampstead, London

9

Fishmongers Arms, Woodgreen

16

Marquee Club, Soho, London

19

Cellar Club, Kingston, Surrey

27

Ram Jam Club, Brixton, London

27

Flamingo Club, Soho, London (all-nighter)

SEPTEMBER 1966

Further recordings at Mayfair

1966

Sound Studios for their debut album.

2

Bluesville, Manor House, London

4

Ricky Tick, Windsor, Berkshire

15

Gaumont Cinema, Hanley

16

Hermitage Halls, Hitchin, Herts

17

Grantham (venue unknown)

18

Blue Moon Club, Hayes, Middlesex

19

Woking (venue unknown)

23

Corn Exchange, Newbury

26

Star Club, Star Hotel, Croydon

27

Marquee Club, Soho, London

30

Ricky Tick, Hounslow

OCTOBER 1966

October saw the release of Cream's first single, "Wrapping Paper" backed with "Cat's Squirrel."

Eric Clapton: **When we made "Wrapping Paper" we didn't think it would harm the image and personally I haven't had any real protests. We knew some people would like it and some wouldn't.**

Jack Bruce: **We did it because we didn't want people to put us into a category straight away. We play soft numbers on stage, maybe we'll change it next time.**

1

Regent Polytechnic, London

Historic gig where Jimi Hendrix joins Cream for an electrifying version of Howlin' Wolf's "Killing Floor."

Eric Clapton: **He became a soul mate for me and musically, what I wanted to hear.**

2

Kirklevington (venue unknown, possibly cancelled)

3

Chester (venue unknown, possibly cancelled)

4

Fishmongers Arms, Woodgreen (possibly cancelled)

5

Reading (venue unknown, possibly cancelled)

6

York (venue unknown, possibly cancelled)

8

Kings College University, Brighton, Sussex

9

Birdcage, Portsmouth

11

Flamingo Club, Soho, London

21

Bluesville 66, Manor House, London

NOVEMBER 1966

3

Ram Jam Club, Brixton, London

4

Wembley TV studios for debut appearance on *Ready Steady Go*

5

Town Hall, East Ham, London

7

Gosport (venue unknown)

8

Marquee Club, Soho, London

9

BBC Studios, London

Live radio session. Numbers recorded: "Wrapping Paper," "Sweet Wine," "Steppin' Out."

11

Public Baths, Sutton

12

Liverpool University, Liverpool

13

Coathams Hotel, Redcar

15

Klooks Kleek, West Hampstead, London

18

Village Hall, Hoverton

19

Blue Moon Club, Cheltenham

25

California Ballroom, Dunstable

DECEMBER 1966

December saw the release of "I Feel Free" backed with "NSU," the band's second single, as well as *Fresh Cream,* its first album.

Eric Clapton: **I am not happy about it as it could have been better. We were working on it so long ago and we have greatly improved since then. I'm not completely happy with the production.**

2

Hornsey Art College, Hornsey

3

Birdcage, Portsmouth

4

Starlite Ballroom, Greenford

5

Baths Hall, Ipswich

7

Hull University, Hull

9

Bluesville 66, Manor House, London

1967

Also, during the day, they record for the BBC.
BBC Radio Studios, London Live radio session. Numbers recorded: "Cat's Squirrel," "Traintime," "Lawdy Mama," "I'm So Glad."

10
Polytechnic, Isleworth

12
Cooks Ferry Inn, Edmonton

13
Exeter University, Exeter, Devon

14
Bromel Club, Bromley Court Hotel, Bromley, Kent

15
Sussex University, Sussex

19
Camberly (venue unknown)

22
Pavilion, Worthing

23
Birmingham (venue unknown)

30
Roundhouse, Chalk Farm, London

JANUARY 1967
7
Ricky Tick, Windsor, Berkshire

10
Marquee Club, Soho, London
Also, during the day, they record for the BBC.
BBC Radio Studios, London. Live session. Numbers recorded: "Four Until Late," "I Feel Free," "NSU."

Top, right: Cream, with well wishers, leaves Heathrow Airport for Los Angeles, August 20, 1967. (BBC)

Far right: On the streets of Soho in 1967. (Dezo Hoffman)

13
Guildhall, Southampton

14
Coventry (venue unknown)

15
Ricky Tick, Hounslow

18
Town Hall, Stourbridge

19
Granby Hall, Leiceister

20
Club A Go Go, Newcastle

21
Floral Hall, Southport

24
Corn Exchange, Bristol

25
BBC *Top of the Pops* television

28
Ram Jam Club, Brixton, London

FEBRUARY 1967
2
Queens Hall, Leeds

4
Technical College, Ewell

5
Saville Theatre, London

9
City Hall, Salisbury

10
Bluesville 66, Manor House, London

11
Baths Pavilion, Matlock

15
Assembly Hall, Aylesbury

18
Tofts Club, Folkestone

19
Starlite Ballroom, Wembley

22
Bromel Club, Bromley Court Hotel, Bromley, Kent

24
Beat Club, Bremen, Germany

25
Star Club, Hamburg, Germany

26
Star Club, Kiel, Germany

MARCH 1967
6
KB Halle, Copenhagen

7
Konserthuset, Stockholm
   Radio broadcast. Tracks:
"NSU," "Steppin' Out," "Traintime," "Toad," "I'm So Glad."

8
Gothenburg, Sweden (venue unknown)

21
Marquee Club, Soho, London
   Cream goes to America for the first time.

25, 26, 27, 28, 29, 30, 31
RKO 58th Street Theater, New York

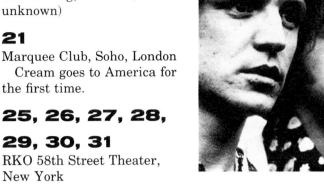

APRIL 1967
1, 2, 3
RKO 58th Street Theater, New York
   Cream performs for ten days, five times a day, on *Murray the K Show* along with various other popular bands of the day: The Who, Lovin' Spoonful, Mitch Ryder, and Wilson Pickett.

Ben Palmer (Cream's road manager): It was a big bill, a lot of acts, and it was supposed to be five shows a day. I think the first curtain was at ten in the morning—the kids were on holiday—and the last show would go on not far short of midnight, and that was for the supper crowd coming out of the theaters."

After the shows Cream goes to Atlantic's New York Studios to begin recording its second album *Disraeli Gears*.

6
Simon Dee Show, London (television)
   Cream mimes to "Strange Brew" with live vocal by Eric.

14
Ricky Tick, Newbury

22
Ricky Tick, Hounslow

MAY 1967
7
Wembley Empire Pool,

1967

Right: Psychedelia exerts an influence over Cream. (Karl Ferris)

DISRAELI GEARS

UK Reaction 593003
US Atco 33-232
Released November 1967

Side One:
1. Strange Brew
2. Sunshine of Your Love
3. World of Pain
4. Dance the Night Away
5. Blue Condition

Side Two:
6. Tales of Brave Ulysses
7. Swlabr
8. We're Going Wrong
9. Outside Woman Blues
10. Take It Back
11. Mother's Lament

Wembley, London (NME Poll Winners Concert). Cream plays two numbers, "NSU" and "I'm So Glad."

20

Berlin Stadium, Berlin

23

Marquee Club, Soho, London

27

Pembroke College May Ball, Oxford

29

Tulip Bulb Auction Hall, Spalding

30

BBC Radio Studios, London
   Live session. Numbers recorded: "Strange Brew,"

"Tales of Brave Ulysses," "We're Going Wrong," "Take It Back."

JUNE 1967

"Strange Brew" backed with "Tales of Brave Ulysses" released as single.

1

Palais Des Sports, Paris

3

Ram Jam Club, Brixton, London

11

Starlite Ballroom, Greenford
   A short tour of Germany followed in such places as Bremen and Braunschweig. Exact dates and venues are not known.

25

Abbey Road Studios, London. Eric joins Mick Jagger, Marianne Faithfull, Keith Richards, Keith Moon, Graham Nash, Pattie Harrison, and Jane Asher, among others, for the BBC *Our World* program broadcast of The Beatles performing "All You Need Is Love." Approximately 400 million people across the world saw the event live on their television screens.

30

Bluesville 67, Manor House, London

JULY 1967

Cream starts recording new material for possible release as single or for use on a future album at IBC Studios in London.

2

Saville Theatre, London (support is the Jeff Beck Group)

12

Floral Hall, Southport
   A short tour of Scotland followed including dates at McGoos in Glasgow, Two Red Shoes in Elgin, and Beach Ballroom in Aberdeen.

AUGUST 1967

More recordings at IBC Studios in London.

13

Seventh National Jazz and Blues Festival, Windsor

17

The Speakeasy, London
Cream headed off to America on August 20 for its first tour.
Cream's set list at this time would normally run as follows: "Tales of Brave Ulysses," "Sunshine of Your Love," "NSU," "Sitting on Top of The World," "Sweet Wine," "Spoonful," "Steppin' Out," "Traintime," "Toad."

22, 23, 24, 25, 26, 27, 29, 30, 31

Fillmore Auditorium, San Francisco

SEPTEMBER 1967
1, 2, 3

Fillmore Auditorium, San Francisco

Jack Bruce: **We'd just been doing three, four, five minute versions of our songs before we went out to San Francisco, and we were very, very nervous because this was something really big for us and also it was almost the first time we had played to a full house. But all these kids had actually come to see us and it was the first time we'd had our own audience on that scale, and they were just shouting things like "Just play anything . . . just play . . . we love you" and stuff, and the whole thing ended up with us just playing these incredibly long improvised things. We became known for that I suppose, and that was how it started, and it was the best time for the group.**

4, 5, 6

Whisky A Go Go, Los Angeles

7

Psychedelic Supermarket, Boston

8

Cross Town Bus Club, Boston

9

Brandeis University, Waltham
After these shows Cream goes to Atlantic's New York Studios to continue recording for its next album, *Wheels of Fire.*

Eric Clapton: **We'll be making tracks, and if something appears that's suitable, it may be put out as a single. But we won't allocate any special time to making singles now.**

Eric also contributed a guitar solo to Aretha Franklin's "Good to Me as I Am to You" at the same time.
Cream also plays several club dates in New York.
The band's set list for its upcoming tour would normally run as follows: "Tales of Brave Ulysses," "NSU," "Sitting on Top of the World," "Sweet Wine," "Rollin' and Tumblin'," "Spoonful," "Steppin' Out," "Traintime," "Toad," "I'm So Glad."
Eric's playing during this tour was particularly wild, including many feedback solos played inches from his Marshall stacks.

23

Village Theater, New York

26, 27, 28, 29, 30

Cafe Au Go Go, New York

OCTOBER 1967
1, 3, 4, 5, 6, 7, 8

Cafe Au Go Go, New York

11, 12

The 5th Dimension Club, Ann Arbor

13, 14, 15

Grande Ballroom, Dearborn
Cream returns to England to play a short tour.

24

BBC Radio Studios, London
Live session. Numbers recorded: "Outside Woman Blues," "Born Under a Bad Sign," "Take It Back."

29

Saville Theatre, London

NOVEMBER 1967

Cream's second album *Disraeli Gears* is released.

Eric Clapton: **We used Atlantic's New York studios. It's done quicker there, we get a better sound, and there's a really hip engineer [Tom Dowd] . . . one of the best in America.**

Tom Dowd: **On *Disraeli Gears*, I remember Eric using a wah wah pedal and a pair of Marshalls turned all the way up. They recorded at ear-shattering level.**

6

Silver Blades Ice Rink, Streatham
A Scandinavian tour followed. Exact dates and cities not known.

23

Club A Go Go, Newcastle

24

Central Pier Ballroom, Morecambe

26

Television appearance on BBC's *Twice a Fortnight* show.

28

Marquee Club, Soho, London

DECEMBER 1967

Eric plays on a session for George Harrison's *Wonderwall* film project. The track he plays on is called "Skiing."

1

Top Rank, Brighton
Toward the end of December, Cream plays a special private concert for a debutante's ball in Chicago.

20

Private party for Chicago ball.

22, 23

Grande Ballroom, Detroit

1968

Top, near right: (Jan Persson)

Top, far right: In the dressing room. (LFI)

Below, far right: (David Redfern)

Bottom: Backstage with Cream. (Chris Walter)

JANUARY 1968

9

BBC Radio Studios, London
  Live session. Numbers recorded: "Politician," "Steppin' Out," "Swlabr," "Blue Condition."

27

St Mary's College, Twickenham

FEBRUARY 1968

Cream plays two shows at the Falkoner Hall in Copenhagen as well as taking part in a short Danish film titled *On a Saturday Night*. The band is filmed playing on the back of a truck along with various other musicians on strings and percussion instruments.

Returning from Denmark, Cream goes to America for its longest tour to date as well as putting the final touches to its next album, *Wheels of Fire*.

Cream's set list for the upcoming tour would normally run as follows: "Tales of Brave Ulysses," "Sunshine of Your Love," "NSU," "I'm Sitting on Top of the World," "Steppin' Out," "Traintime," "Toad," "I'm So Glad."

23
Civic Auditorium, Santa Monica (2 shows)

29
Winterland Auditorium, San Francisco (2 shows)
 Live recording

MARCH 1968
1, 2
Winterland Auditorium, San Francisco (2 shows nightly)
 Live recording

3, 7
Fillmore Auditorium, San Francisco (2 shows nightly)
 Live recording

8, 9, 10
Winterland Auditorium, San Francisco (2 shows nightly)
 Live recording

Left: On tour with Cream in Scandinavia. (Jan Persson x 3)

Bottom left: (John Shepherd)

Overleaf
Left: On the streets of Soho. (Alec Byrne/Relay Photos)

Right: With an elderly admirer in Hyde Park. (Alex Byrne/Relay Photos)

27

1968

WHEELS OF FIRE

UK Polydor 583031/2
US Atco SD 2-700
Released August 1968

Side One:
1. White Room
2. Sitting on Top of the World
3. Passing the Time
4. As You Said

Side Two:
5. Pressed Rat and Warthog
6. Politician
7. Those Were the Days
8. Born Under a Bad Sign
9. Deserted Cities of the Heart

Side Three:
10. Crossroads
11. Spoonful

Side Four:
12. Traintime
13. Toad

Right: Performing with Cream at their Farewell Concert at London's Royal Albert Hall, November 26, 1968. (Barry Plummer)

11
Memorial Auditorium, Sacramento

15, 16, 17
Shrine Auditorium, Los Angeles

18
Convention Center, Anaheim

19
The Family Dog, Denver

20
Eric busted on marijuana charge alongside Neil Young, Richie Furay, and Jim Messina at Joni Mitchell's house.

21
Beloit College, Beloit, Wisconsin

22
Clowes Hall, Butler University, Indianapolis

23
Brown University, Providence

27
Staples High School, Westport, Conn.

29
Hunter College Auditorium, New York

30
Convention Center, Dallas

31
Music Hall, Houston

APRIL 1968

5
Back Bay Theater, Boston

6
Commodore Ballroom, Lowell

7
Eastman College Theater, Rochester

8
Capitol Theater, Ottawa

12, 13, 14
Electric Factory, Philadelphia

16
Paul Suave Arena, Montreal

19, 20, 21
Grande Ballroom, Dearborn

22
Massey Hall, Toronto

27
Coliseum, Chicago
Cream interrupts its tour for a short break. Pressures mount and rumors of a split are reported in the music press.

Eric Clapton: **All rumors are denied. I'm happy with the group, although needless to say there has been strain. We've been doing two and a half months of one-nighters and that is the hardest I've ever worked in my life. Financially and popularity wise we're doing unbelievably well in America.**

MAY 1968

Cream's fourth single "Anyone for Tennis" backed with "Pressed Rat and Warthog" is released.

5
New City Opera House, St. Paul

12
Music Hall, Cleveland

14
Veterans Memorial Auditorium, Columbus

17, 18
Convention Center, Anaheim

19
Exhibit Hall, San Diego

20
Smothers Brothers Comedy Hour television taping in Los Angeles. Cream mimes to its

new single "Anyone for Tennis" and also performs an explosive live version of "Sunshine of Your Love."

24
Robertson Gym, University of California, Santa Barbara

25
Civic Auditorium, San Jose

27
Swing Auditorium, San Bernardino

28
Pacific Center, Long Beach

29
Eagles Auditorium, Seattle

31
Calgary Stampede, Calgary

JUNE 1968
Cream adds final overdubs on *Wheels of Fire*

1
Sales Pavilion Annex, Edmonton

2
PNE Coliseum, Vancouver

7, 8
Grande Ballroom, Dearborn

14
Island Garden, West Hempstead, Long Island

15
Oakdale Music Theater, Wallingford, Connecticut

16
Camden Music Fair, Camden, New Jersey

After the tour ends it is announced that Cream will break up after a farewell tour of both America and England.

Eric Clapton: **I've been on the road seven years and I'm going on a big holiday.**

Robert Stigwood: **Cream are going to follow their individual musical policies.**

It is fair to say that, at the height of the band's career, Cream ignored England, and fan reaction was one of anger and sadness.

Melody Maker: **Goodbye Eric, Jack and Ginger. We dug your sound, but you kicked us in the teeth.**

On his return to England, Eric took part in a session for Jackie Lomax at George Harrison's request. Jackie's album is to be called *Is This What You Want.*

Another session Eric took part in around this time was for a lady named Martha Velez, whose brother played congas with Jimi Hendrix's short-lived Gypsy, Sun and Rainbows band. Her album is to be called *Fiends and Angels.*

AUGUST 1968
Wheels of Fire, a double album, is released. Half is from studio sessions and the other is recorded live at the Winterland and Fillmore West in San Francisco.

By this time, however, Eric was under the spell of The Band's *Music From Big Pink.*

Eric Clapton: **I think this music will influence a lot of people. Everybody I have played it to has flipped. The Band is releasing an album called *Music From Big Pink.* Since I heard all this stuff all my values have changed. I think it has probably influenced me."**

Cream takes a few months off before undertaking its farewell tour.

SEPTEMBER 1968
Cream's fifth single released, "Sunshine of Your Love" backed with "Swlabr." It reaches number five in the American charts which shows how popular the group is there, thanks to its heavy touring; but it only reaches the UK top thirty.

During this break, Eric

Above: The view from the audience at the Royal Albert Hall Farewell show. (Barry Plummer)

31

1968

continued his session work for his friend George Harrison on recordings for The Beatles and Doris Troy.

Eric was to participate in more and more guest appearances over the years and continues to this day.

6

Abbey Road Studios, London. Eric plays a guitar solo on "While My Guitar Gently Weeps" for George Harrison. The track will appear on The Beatles *White Album*.

OCTOBER 1968

Cream records its final studio tracks at IBC Studios, London for its proposed last album. The idea was to have a double again, consisting of one new studio album and one which would be recorded on Cream's farewell tour. George Harrison joined Eric for the recording of "Badge."

Cream starts its farewell tour of America. The set performed for this tour would normally run as follows:

"White Room," "Politician," "Crossroads," "Sunshine of Your Love," "Spoonful," "Deserted Cities of the Heart," "Toad," "I'm So Glad," "Sitting on Top of the World," "Traintime."

4

Alameda County Coliseum, Oakland
   Live recording

5

University of New Mexico, Albuquerque

7

Civic Opera House, Chicago

11

Arena, New Haven

12

Olympia Stadium, Detroit

13

Chicago Coliseum, Chicago

14

Veterans Memorial Auditorium, Des Moines

18, 19

The Forum, Los Angeles
   Live recording

20

Sports Arena, San Diego
   Live recording

24

Sam Houston Coliseum, Houston

25

Memorial Auditorium, Dallas

26

Sports Arena, Miami

27

Chastain Park Amphitheater, Atlanta

31

Boston Garden, Boston

NOVEMBER 1968

1

The Spectrum, Philadelphia

2

Madison Square Garden, New York

GOODBYE

UK Polydor 583053
US Atco SD 7001
Released March 1969

Side One:
1. I'm So Glad
2. Politician
Side Two:
3. Sitting on Top of the World
4. Badge
5. Doing That Scrapyard Thing
6. What a Bringdown

Right: At the Rolling Stones' Rock And Roll Circus, Wembley, December 10 & 11, 1968. Left to right, back row: John Entwistle, Keith Moon; front row: Yoko Ono, Julian Lennon, John Lennon, Eric Clapton, Brian Jones. (Andre Csillag)

Opposite page: Eric photographed by Lord Snowdon during 1969.

Above: Rehearsing at Eric's home near Guildford with Rick Grech and Steve Winwood for Blind Faith. (Robert Stigwood Organization)

Cream receives platinum records for sales of over $2 million for *Wheels of Fire*. The award is made on stage at Madison Square Garden.

3

Civic Center Arena, Baltimore

4

Rhode Island Auditorium, Providence
 Last US show before heading back to England

26

Royal Albert Hall, London
 Cream performs to two sold-out shows. Its last ever concerts consisted of: "White Room," "Politician," "I'm So Glad," "Sitting on Top of the World," "Crossroads," "Toad," "Spoonful," "Sunshine of Your Love," "Steppin' Out." The shows were filmed by Tony Palmer for broadcast by BBC Television in early 1969. The show was eventually released in a reduced format for the home video market as *Farewell Cream.*

Eric Clapton: We haven't played here for . . . well I don't know how long . . . over a year, and I had no idea we were so popular. I was amazed we played to such full houses. I didn't think anybody would remember us . . . it was really a fine evening for me, and I felt very exited.

Eric plays a Gibson Firebird for the first show and a Gibson ES335 for the second.

DECEMBER 1968
10, 11

Intertel Studios, Wembley
 Eric takes part in the *Rock and Roll Circus* film, an entertainment extravaganza put on by The Rolling Stones. Artists appearing include The Who, Jethro Tull, Taj Mahal, and Winston Legtheigh and the Dirty Macs (consisting of John Lennon, Yoko Ono, Mitch Mitchell, Keith Richards, Ivry Gitlis, and Eric Clapton).
 Cream performs two numbers on film, "Yer Blues" and "Yoko Jam."

December also marks the end of Traffic. Eric and Stevie Winwood get together for informal jams with the possibility of forming a band.

JANUARY 1969

Cream's sixth single released: "White Room" backed with "Those Were the Days."
 Melody Maker prints a news item stating "Eric Clapton and Stevie Winwood may join forces with two members of the late Otis Redding's backing band to record an album."

Robin Turner: It is true that Eric and Stevie have discussed forming a group together and that Eric, while on the Cream's tour of America, did discuss it with Otis Redding's drummer and bass player. But plans are still very fluid at the moment.

Al Jackson was the drummer and did get to record with Eric finally in 1974, for the *461 Ocean Boulevard* sessions. The bass player was Duck Dunn, who also got to record with Eric as well as joining him for many years in his band. (*Money and Cigarettes* and *Behind the Sun* are the albums on which he plays.)

FEBRUARY 1969

Eric Clapton: I don't know whether I'll be doing an album of mine, or an album of mine and Stevie's, or just Stevie's album. It will just have to sort itself out because I can't be bothered making those kind of decisions beforehand.

Eric and Stevie begin formal rehearsals and recording at Morgan Studios in London. Ginger Baker was back with Eric at Stevie's specific request. Recording lasted till June.

Eric Clapton: As far as Stevie Winwood, Ginger Baker, and myself are concerned we are just jamming and we have no definite plans for the future.

MARCH 1969

Jackie Lomax releases his *Is This What You Want* album which features Eric on several tracks.

18

Staines television studios. Eric takes part in a supersession for a film called *Supershow*.
 Eric, Jack Bruce, Roland Kirk, Jon Hiesman, Dick Heckstall-Smith, Ron Burton, and Vernon Martin perform an instrumental called "Slate 69." Eric also joins Buddy Guy for the first time for a version of "Everything Gonna Be Alright."

APRIL 1969

Eric plays on a session for Billy Preston.
 Cream's seventh single released: "Badge" backed with "What a Bringdown."
 The music press announce that the new band will be giving a free concert in London's Hyde Park on June 7 followed by a Scandinavian tour and then a U.S. tour.

Left and above: Blind Faith's free concert in Hyde Park, June 7, 1969. (Barry Wentzell & Michael Putland/Retna.)

MAY 1969

Eric Clapton: We've been in the studios most of the time and done several songs . . . one of mine, two by Dylan, one by Buddy Holly, and one by Steve. We've got enough to release two albums already.

Melody Maker exclusively reveals the name of the new supergroup . . . Blind Faith.
 Bassist Rick Grech, late of Family, joins the other three at Olympic Studios for recording sessions of Blind Faith's first album.

JUNE 1969

Martha Velez's *Fiends and Angels* album released.
 Blind Faith's first record release is a studio instrumental issued by Island Records in a limited run of 500 to inform clients of their change of address. Needless to say, this is a highly sought after collectors' item as it has never had a general release. However, it did receive the compact disc treatment in 1992 when it was issued on a Westwood One radio-only promo titled *Eric Clapton—Rarities on Compact Disc, Vol. II.*

1969

Top, far right: Eric with girlfriend Alice Ormsby Gore. (BBC)

Top, near right: Rehearsing at home with Blind Faith. (LFI)

Bottom, far right: With Delaney and Bonnie Bramlett at Heathrow Airport, November 10, 1969. (BBC)

BLIND FAITH

UK Polydor 583059
US Atco SD 33-304
Released August 1969

Side One:
1. Had to Cry Today
2. Can't Find My Way Home
3. Well All Right
4. Presence of the Lord
Side Two:
5. Sea of Joy
6. Do What You Like

7

Hyde Park, London

World premiere of Blind Faith. They perform a sixty-five-minute set consisting of "Well All Right," "Sea of Joy," "Sleeping in the Ground," "Under My Thumb," "Can't Find My Way Home," "Do What You Like," "In the Presence of the Lord," "Means to an End," and "Had to Cry Today." The whole concert is filmed and recorded.

"Well All Right" was shown on a Bee Gees television special called *Cucumber Castle.* Unfortunately, it was overdubbed with the studio version and not the live sound!

Eric plays a Fender Telecaster Custom with a blond Stratocaster neck for the concert.

Rick Grech: **I was nervous at Hyde Park . . . I think everybody was. We knew the numbers but not to the extent of not having to think about them. I'm sure the majority of the audience expected the band to sound like Cream, and that's not the way it is. Cream were three virtuosos . . . all improvising. We're not out to outsolo each other.**

A short Scandinavian tour followed.

JULY 1969

Blind Faith goes to America amid press and fan hysteria for the arrival of the world's biggest "supergroup."

However, the tour turns out to be a disaster because the majority of the shows are marred by violence between fans and police, and because fans would give the band standing ovations before even hearing a note. Blind Faith indeed!

On the tour they were supported by Free, and Delaney and Bonnie. Their set would normally consist of: "Had to Cry Today," "Can't Find My Way Home," "Sleeping in the Ground," "Well All Right," "In the Presence of the Lord," "Means to an End," "Do What You Like," "Crossroads," and "Sunshine of Your Love."

"Sunshine" would normally include Delaney and Bonnie.

12

Madison Square Garden, New York

13

Kennedy Center, Bridgeport

16

The Spectrum, Philadelphia

18

Varsity Stadium, Toronto

20

Civic Center, Baltimore

26

County Stadium, Milwaukee

27

International Amphitheater,
Chicago

AUGUST 1969

1

Olympia Stadium, Detroit

3

Kiel Stadium, St. Louis

8

Seattle Center Stadium,
Seattle

9

PNE Coliseum, Vancouver

10

Memorial Coliseum, Portland

14

Alameda County Coliseum,
Oakland

15

The Forum, Los Angeles
   The Los Angeles show
epitomized the violent aspects
of the tour. The Forum's

house lights were turned on
three times during the set to
enable police to pursue crowd
members. A row of security
guards lined the front of the
stage like a football team
ready for any event. However,
despite the obvious problems,
Blind Faith played well and
the crowd left happy.

Eric Clapton: **The violence
happened everywhere we
played. The worst were Los
Angeles, New York, and
Phoenix. When I was with
Cream it had not really grown
then. Now kids come to a
show with one idea . . .
violence and to heckle the
cops.**

16

Arena, Santa Barbara

19

Sam Houston Coliseum,
Houston

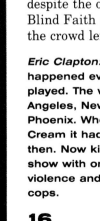

Bottom left: On tour with
Delaney and Bonnie, 1969.
(LFI)

1969

20
Hemisfair Arena, San Antonio

22
Salt Palace, Salt Lake City

23
Memorial Coliseum, Phoenix

24
HIC Arena, Honolulu

Blind Faith's eponymous album is released. Advance orders had reached half a million.

Press controversy is caused because the group's album cover features a nude eleven-year-old girl holding a silver spaceship. As a result, many shops refuse to handle the LP in America and Atco are forced to release an alternate sleeve.

Ahmet Ertegun (president of Atlantic Records): We haven't withdrawn the other by any means . . . we have just given people a choice. After all we aren't in the art business.

Robert Stigwood (manager): We just liked the design.

As the tour progressed, Eric spent more and more time with the support band, Delaney and Bonnie. He eventually ended traveling from the gigs with them in their tour bus.

Delaney Bramlett: The first time I met Eric was after the first show at New York's Madison Square Garden. We passed the time of day and got talking. We realized we both admired the same people, particularly Robert Johnson, and we both had an almost identical collection of records. The only difference was that I had been raised on this music, while Eric had raised himself on it.

By the end of the tour, Eric was ready to throw in the towel. Blind Faith was not given the chance to mature by fans, the media, and even the band members themselves.

Top and bottom right: With Delaney and Bonnie at the Royal Albert Hall, December 1, 1969. (Chris Walter)

Opposite page
Top: With George Harrison on Delaney and Bonnie tour. (*Melody Maker*)

Bottom: Backstage at London's Lyceum Ballroom, December 15, 1969. Back row, left to right: Jim Price, Bobby Keyes, Jim Gordon, Klaus Voorman, Bonnie and Delaney Bramlett; center: George Harrison, unknown, Keith Moon, unknown, Eric Barrett, Billy Preston; front: Tony Ashton, John Lennon, Yoko Ono. (Barry Plummer)

Eric Clapton: I don't think the group is going to stay together very long. Stevie's going to do something on his own and I will do something on my own.

Billy Preston's album *That's the Way God Planned It* is released in August on the Apple label. Eric plays on the title track as well as "Do What You Want To."

SEPTEMBER 1969

At the end of the tour, Eric hung out with Delaney and even participated on the recording of their next single at A&M Studios in Los Angeles. The two tracks he played on were "Comin' Home" and "Groupie (Superstar)." They also started writing some songs together for a possible solo album by Eric.

On his return to London he is invited to participate at a charity concert in Toronto with John Lennon. The group would call themselves the Plastic Ono Band.

13
Varsity Stadium, Toronto

Eric performs with John Lennon (guitar, vocals), Klaus Voorman (bass), Alan White (drums), Yoko Ono (vocals).

They play: "Blue Suede Shoes," "Money," "Dizzy Miss Lizzy," "Yer Blues," "Cold Turkey," "Give Peace a Chance," "Don't Worry Kyoto," "John John."

An amazing concert made all the more remarkable by the fact that this band had not rehearsed other than on the plane on the way over to Canada! The show was filmed and recorded for later release.

Eric Clapton: I didn't know anything about it until I got a call from John and I flew out the next morning. It was a great gig and we played well.

25–28
Abbey Road Studios, London. Eric plays on a session for the new Plastic Ono Band single, "Cold Turkey."

Despite the various diversions, Blind Faith is technically still together while members do their own thing. In fact, they never stop doing their own thing and Blind Faith never play again.

OCTOBER 1969
3–6
Abbey Road Studios, London. Eric plays on another session for the Plastic Ono Band. The track "Don't Worry Kyoto" will be on the flip side of "Cold Turkey."

7
Morgan Studios, London. Eric plays on a session for Rick Grech's upcoming solo album which unfortunately, remains unreleased. Other musicians who played were George Harrison, Alan White, Trevor Burton, Stevie Winwood, and Graham Bond. Two numbers were eventually released as bonus tracks on the European issue of the *Blind Faith* CD, but I would not rush out and buy a copy if I were you.

Toward the end of this month Eric is invited to play on sessions for Leon Russell who is in town recording his new album at Olympic Sound Studios.

Another session Eric played on this month is for Doris Troy alongside George Harrison, Ringo Starr, Steve Stills, Peter Frampton, Billy Preston, Bobby Keys, Jim Price, and Klaus Voorman.

Eric also lays down a guitar track for a Shawn Phillips session at Trident Studios, London.

It is also likely he laid down some guitar parts for a Bobby Keys solo project at this time.

NOVEMBER 1969
Eric starts preliminary recordings for his first solo album at Olympic Studios in Barnes. However, the majority of sessions will in fact take place in Los Angeles later.

10
Delaney and Bonnie arrive at Heathrow Airport, London, where they are met by Eric.

1969/ 1970

Eric Clapton: **After Blind Faith, Delaney and I then got together and wrote a few songs. I thought it would be a good idea to get them over here and suggested it to the Stigwood Organization.**

14

Premiere of *Supershow* film at the Lyceum in London.

Eric rehearses with Delaney and Bonnie for their forthcoming tour.

26

Live recording for *Beat Club* television program in Germany. They play "Comin' Home," "Poor Elijah," and "Where There's a Will There's a Way."

27

Jahrhunderthalle, Frankfurt

28

Congress Halle, Hamburg

29

Sport Palais, Cologne

DECEMBER 1969

1

British Tour opens at the Royal Albert Hall, London.

2

Colston Hall, Bristol (2 shows 6:15 and 8:45)

3

Town Hall, Birmingham (2 shows 6:15 and 8:45)

4

City Hall, Sheffield (2 shows 6:20 and 8:50)

5

City Hall, Newcastle-upon-Tyne (2 shows 6:15 and 8:45)

6

Empire Theatre, Liverpool (2 shows 6:45 and 9:00). George Harrison sings "Everybody's Trying to Be My Baby."

7

Fairfield Hall, Croydon (2 shows 6:15 and 8:35). This show was recorded for later release as "On Tour." The band consisted of: Delaney Bramlett (rhythm guitar, vocals), Bonnie Bramlett (vocals), Eric Clapton (lead guitar, vocals), Dave Mason (guitar), George Harrison (guitar), Carl Radle (bass), Jim Gordon (drums), Bobby Whitlock (organ, vocals), Jim Price (trumpet, trombone), Bobby Keyes (saxophone), Tex Johnson (conga, bongo drums), and Rita Coolidge (vocals).

George Harrison did not play at the Albert Hall show.

George Harrison: **With Delaney and Bonnie there's no expectations because it's really quite anonymous. You just go and do whatever you can do.**

Eric Clapton: **This is the first tour I've ever been on in my life, and I've been on a good few I can tell you, where everybody has had a good time, and there are a lot of people on this tour.**

10, 11, 12

Falkoner Theatre, Copenhagen
(The show on 12 filmed by Danish television for later broadcast.)

15

The Lyceum, London. "Peace for Christmas" show by the Plastic Ono Band featuring John Lennon, Yoko Ono, Delaney and Bonnie, Eric Clapton, Jim Price, Bobby Keys, Jim Gordon, Bobby Whitlock, George Harrison, Alan White, Billy Preston, Legs Larry Smith, and Keith Moon. This amazing band performs "Cold Turkey" and "Don't Worry Kyoto (Mummy's Only Looking for Her Hand in the Snow)."

The show is recorded and released in 1972 as a free album with John and Yoko's "Sometime In New York City."

Plastic Ono Band releases *Live Peace in Toronto* LP. Eric is on all tracks.

Delaney and Bonnie with Eric Clapton release their single "Comin' Home" backed with "Groupie (Superstar)."

Eric plays on a Vivian Stanshall session.

JANUARY 1970

Eric enters Village Recorders, Los Angeles, to record his first solo album under the supervision of Delaney Bramlett. Jerry Allison and Sonny Curtis, both from Buddy Holly's Crickets, give their vocal support on this session. The backing musicians are basically "The Friends" with the addition of John Simon (piano) and Stephen Stills (guitar).

The sessions also produce a track with Atlantic's legendary saxophonist King Curtis called "Teasin" as well as two tracks with The Crickets, "Rocking 50's Rock'n'Roll" and the Buddy Holly classic "That'll Be the Day."

FEBRUARY 1970

Short U.S. tour with Delaney and Bonnie.

2

Massey Hall, Toronto

3, 4, 5

Record Plant, New York. Eric takes part in a super jam which is later released as *Music From Free Creek*. Other musicians involved are Doctor John, Delaney Bramlett, Moogy Kingman, Tommy Cosgrove, and many more.

5

ABC Television Studios, New York. Delaney and Bonnie along with Eric appear on the *Dick Cavett Show* performing "Comin' Home," "Poor Elijah," and "Where There's a Will There's a Way."

6, 7

Fillmore East, New York

8, 9

Tea Party, Boston

11

Electric Factory, Philadelphia (B.B. King jams on the encore)

12

Symphony Hall, Minneapolis

14

Chicago Auditorium, Chicago

15

Memorial Hall, Kansas

19, 20, 21, 22

Fillmore West, San Francisco

MARCH 1970

3

Civic Auditorium, Santa Monica

After the tour ends, Eric returns to England to play on several sessions as a guest. The first of these is for Steve Stills at Island Studios recording "Fishes And Scorpions" and "Go Back Home." He also played on sessions for Jonathan Kelly on a number called "Don't You Believe It" and for Ashton Gardener And Dyke on "I'm Your Spiritual Breadman."

APRIL, MAY 1970

The next session Eric plays on is for one of his heroes, Howlin' Wolf. Other guests include Ringo Starr, Charlie Watts, Klaus Voorman, Ian Stewart, Bill Wyman, and Stevie Winwood.

Another session Eric plays on is for Billy Preston's second album, *Encouraging Words*. It is also probable that he recorded tracks with Jesse Davis at this time.

Meanwhile, back in the U.S., Delaney and Bonnie's Friends had gone their separate ways and joined Joe Cocker's infamous "Mad Dogs and Englishmen" tour. However, after the tour they find themselves at loose ends and come to England at Eric's request to start work on sessions for George Harrison's *All Things Must Pass* triple

album. Eric also participates in these sessions and intends forming a group with Jim Gordon, Carl Radle, and Bobby Whitlock. Rehearsals take place at Eric's country house.

Eric Clapton: **I still get a great deal of satisfaction out of playing on someone else's record or singing in with someone else's group. But so far I'm really very keen to do this. [form Derek and the Dominos].**

JUNE 1970

World premiere of Eric's new band.

14

Derek and the Dominos perform for Dr. Spock's Civil Liberties Legal Defense Fund at the Lyceum in London. Dave Mason is in the band for this show but he leaves to pursue his solo career in the States.

Eric Clapton: **We are knocked out by the way it went. We only had just over a day's rehearsal and yet it was as if we had been together for months.**

The Dominos continue their session work with George Harrison.

Release of *Live Cream* album.

Shawn Phillips releases his *Contribution* LP. Eric plays on "Man Whole Covered Wagon."

Delaney and Bonnie on Tour With Eric Clapton released.

"Don't You Believe It" single by Jonathan Kelly released. Eric plays on A side.

JULY 1970

Derek and the Dominos record "Tell the Truth" and "Roll It Over," augmented by George Harrison during sessions for his upcoming album at Abbey Road studios. Phil Spector produces the track.

Eric also plays guitar for a Dr. John session at Trident Studios in London.

"Teasin" by King Curtis released as a single. Eric plays on A side.

AUGUST 1970

Derek and the Dominos open their first ever tour with Jim Gordon (drums), Carl Radle (bass), Bobby Whitlock (keyboards and vocals), Eric (guitar and vocals).

The basic set normally runs as follows: "Roll It Over," "Blues Power," "Have You Ever Loved a Woman," "Bad Boy," "Country Life," "Anyday," "Bottle of Red Wine," "Don't Know Why," "Tell the Truth."

August also sees the release of Eric's first solo album simply called *Eric Clapton*.

Eric Clapton: **The first track on side one will be the instrumental we did, which was "Just a Good Day" recorded in Los Angeles, when Leon Russell came along. It was just a jam. I'm really pleased with it. It's also matched to another track on the album called "Blues Power" which is a song that Leon wrote. The words are really applicable to me. And then there's "Lonesome and a Long Way From Home," which is a song that Delaney Bramlett wrote a long time ago. He was doing it with King Curtis when I arrived in L.A. and Curtis didn't like his voice on it. Curtis doesn't sing much but he's a great singer. So I said I'd like to do a version of it. The next one, "After Midnight," is a song that J.J. Cale wrote. He's one of those people from Tulsa and I think he's an engineer now. He made a record of it and I dug the record a lot so we did our version of that. "Lovin' You, Lovin' Me" started out as a song that Delaney and Leon wrote for the Blind Faith to do. I liked it very much. I don't know if the others ever heard it. I said I wanted to do it if I ever did a solo album. "I Don't Know Why" is a ballad, a love song kind of thing. It was an idea that Delaney had when he came to England. "Get Up and**

1970

Top right: Derek and the Dominos pictured in Eric's garden. Left to right: Jim Gordon, Carl Radle, Bobby Whitlock, and Eric Clapton. (Robert Stigwood Organization)

Opposite page
Bottom: At London's Lyceum, June 14, 1970. (LFI)

Top left: With Dave Mason at London's Lyceum. (Barry Wentzell)

Bottom left: (SKR)

LIVE CREAM VOL 1

UK Polydor 2382016
US Atco 33328
Released June 1970

S i d e O n e :
1. NSU
2. Sleepy Time
3. Lawdy Mama
S i d e T w o :
4. Sweet Wine
5. Rollin' and Tumblin'

Get Your Man a Bottle of Red Wine" is a ballad too. We were going to the studio one day in L.A. and we had no songs, nothing at all to do. We were getting panicky on the way and we just thought up the song and did it when we got there. It's just a shuffle. "I Told You For the Last Time" is a song that Delaney played on acoustic guitar . . . one of his motel shot numbers I think. We changed that around and arranged it for a big band sort of feel and it came out like a country number really. The last one is called "She Rides." That just came from the lyrics of the original song we wrote. But when we went into the studio, the track came off so well that we abandoned the original song and since then I've been trying to think up a set of lyrics to go with the track. That's what has been holding the album up.

The song eventually was titled "Let It Rain."

1
Roundhouse, Dagenham

2
The Place, Hanley, Stoke-on-Trent

7
Mecca, Newcastle-upon-Tyne

8
California, Dunstable

9
Mothers, Birmingham

11
Marquee Club, London

12
Speakeasy, London

14
Winter Gardens, Malvern

15
Tofts, Folkestone

16
Black Prince, Bexley

18
The Pavilion, Bournemouth

21
Town Hall, Torquay

22
Van Dyke Club, Plymouth.

23
Derek and the Dominos fly out to Miami to record at

Criteria Studios under the supervision of Tom Dowd.

Tom Dowd: **When I finished doing the 'Layla' album, I walked out of the studio and said, "That's the best goddamn record I've made in ten years."**

Thanks to Tom Dowd, Eric is introduced to Duane Allman. Both guitarists had admired each other from a distance and when they met it was as if they were long lost brothers. Eric immediately asked Duane along to the Criteria sessions.

Duane Allman: **We were playing together and singing a lot acoustically and we got on very well together, like a sort of Laurel and Hardy singing the blues. He came to one of our gigs and that is how I got to know him. He is the only guitarist in London that seems to know what he is doing, and he freaked out when he heard our band. He invited us to go to the studio to play around and that's where it started. I am going to join Eric's band for a few dates towards the end of his tour.**

At the end of the sessions

Derek and the Dominos return to the U.K. to continue their tour and play some new numbers which they have just recorded. Their new set usually runs as follows: "Why Does Love Got to Be So Sad," "Tell the Truth," "Blues Power," "Have You Ever Loved a Woman," "Keep on Growing," "Nobody Knows You When You're Down and Out," "Bottle of Red Wine," "Little Wing," "Roll It Over," "Bell Bottom Blues," and "Let It Rain."

Derek and the Dominos release their first single "Tell the Truth" backed with "Roll It Over." It is withdrawn at the last minute because of the group's dissatisfaction with the recording.

Group spokesman: The group rerecorded ''Tell the Truth'' during their studio time in Miami, for inclusion on their new double album. When they compared the two they were so unhappy about the original that they asked Polydor if they could withdraw it. We suggested ''After Midnight'' as a single because of pressure from DJs and fans.

SEPTEMBER 1970
20
Fairfield Hall, Croydon

21
De Montford Hall, Leicester

22
Eric flies out to Paris and jams with Buddy Guy and Junior Wells, who are supporting the Rolling Stones at L'Olympia. Eric flies back the next day.

1970

All shots from Croydon Fairfield Halls, September 20, 1970. (Barry Plummer)

ERIC CLAPTON

UK Polydor 2383021
US Atco SD 33329
Released August 1970

Side One:
1. Slunky
2. Bad Boy
3. Told You for the Last Time
4. After Midnight
5. Easy Now
6. Blues Power

Side Two:
7. Bottle of Red Wine
8. Lovin' You Lovin' Me
9. Lonesome and a Long Way From Home
10. Don't Know Why
11. Let It Rain

23
Dome, Brighton

24
Philharmonic Hall, Liverpool

25
Greens Playhouse, Glasgow

27
Colston Hall, Bristol

28
Free Trade Hall, Manchester. Billy Preston releases his *Encouraging Words* LP. Eric plays on "Right Now" and "Encouraging Words."

OCTOBER 1970

2
College of Technology, Nottingham

3
Lads Club, Norwich

4
Coatham Bowl, Redcar

5
Town Hall, Birmingham. Robert Plant is due to jam, but when he comes on stage one of the road crew ushers him off, not having recognized him.

7
Winter Gardens, Bournemouth

8
University, Leeds

9
Penthouse, Scarborough

11
Lyceum, London. This was the last U.K. show before flying to the U.S. for a long tour.

Chris Charlesworth (in Melody Maker): **When Eric Clapton flew across the Atlantic on Tuesday, his ears were probably still ringing with the applause he collected at London's Lyceum on Sunday. A tighter unit would be hard to find.**

13
Derek and the Dominos fly to New York for the start of their American tour. The set list would consist of the following: "Got to Get Better in a Little While," "Blues Power/ Have You Ever Loved a Woman," "Key to the Highway," "Tell the Truth," "Nobody Knows You When You're Down and Out," "Let It Rain," "Why Does Love Got to Be So Sad," "Presence of the Lord," "Bottle of Red Wine," "Roll It Over," "Little Wing," "Crossroads," "Sweet Little Rock 'n' Roller," "Stormy Monday," "Little Queenie." Eric also adds final overdubs to the "Layla" tracks recorded back in September, and finds time to participate in sessions for Buddy Guy and Junior Wells as well as James Luther Dickinson.

15
Rider College, Trenton

16, 17
Electric Factory Theater, Philadelphia

21
Lisner Auditorium, Washington

23, 24

illmore East, New York.
hows recorded for later
elease.

29

leinhalls Music Hall, Buffalo

30

lbany State University
ymnasium, Albany

31

ome, Virginia Beach, Va.
After Midnight" backed with
Easy Now" released as a
ingle.

NOVEMBER 1970

ivic Auditorium,
acksonville

5

ohnny Cash TV show,
ashville. Eric plays "It's Too
ate," "Got to Get Better in a
ittle While," and "Blues
ower," and is joined by
ohnny Cash and Carl
erkins for a rousing version
f "Matchbox."

6

McFarlin Auditorium, Dallas

7

Community Center Theater,
San Antonio

13

University of Nevada, Reno

14

Fairgrounds Coliseum, Salt
Lake City

17

Memorial Auditorium,
Sacramento

18, 19

Community Theater, Berkeley

20

Civic Auditorium, Santa
Monica

21

Civic Auditorium, Pasadena

22

Community Concourse, San
Diego

25

Auditorium Theater, Chicago

26

Music Hall, Cincinnati
  B. B. King jams on
"Everyday I Have the Blues."

27

Kiel Opera House, St. Louis

28

Music Hall, Cleveland

29

Painters Mill Music Fair,
Owings Mills, Md.
George Harrison releases his
triple album *All Things Must
Pass.* Eric plays on "Wah
Wah," "Isn't It a Pity (version
one)," "What Is Life," "Run of
the Mill," "Beware of
Darkness," "Awaiting on You
All," "Plug Me In," "I
Remember Jeep," and
"Thanks for the Pepperoni."

DECEMBER 1970

1

Curtis Hixon Hall, Tampa.
Duane Allman joins Derek

**LAYLA AND OTHER
ASSORTED LOVE
SONGS**

UK Polydor 2625005
US Atco SD 2704
Released December 1970

S i d e O n e :
1. I Looked Away
2. Bell Bottom Blues
3. Keep On Growing
4. Nobody Knows You When
   You're Down and Out
S i d e T w o :
5. I Am Yours
6. Anyday
7. Key to the Highway
S i d e T h r e e :
8. Tell the Truth
9. Why Does Love Got to Be
   So Sad
10. Have You Ever Loved a
    Woman
S i d e F o u r :
11. Little Wing
12. It's Too Late
13. Layla
14. Thorn Tree in the Garden

and the Dominos for a couple of shows.

2
War Memorial Auditorium, Syracuse. With Duane Allman.

3
East Town Theater, Detroit

4, 5
Capitol Theater, Portchester, NY.

6
Suffolk Community College, Selden, N.Y.
Last ever Dominos gig.

18
Olympic Sound Studios, Barnes, London. Eric joins the Rolling Stones for a recording of "Brown Sugar."

Al Kooper: They cajoled Eric Clapton, myself and Bobby Keys to join them in a previously unheard tune called "Brown Sugar." But the version on "Sticky Fingers" is another one entirely.

JANUARY 1971
Eric attends premiere of Joe Cocker's *Mad Dogs and Englishmen* film at the Empire, Leicester Square, London.
   Eric plays on sessions for a Bobby Whitlock solo project at Olympic Sound Studios in Barnes, London. He also over-dubs some guitar solos for a John Mayall project at IBC Studios in London.

FEBRUARY 1971
8
Eric returns to Criteria Studios, Miami, to complete work on the Buddy Guy and Junior Wells album.

Eric Clapton: What we have left is mainly mixing and a little repolishing.

The Crickets release their *Rockin' 50's Rock 'n' Roll* LP. Eric plays on "Rockin' 50's Rock 'n' Roll" and "That'll Be the Day."

APRIL 1971
Jesse Davis releases his solo LP. Eric plays on "Reno Street Incident," "Tulsa County," "Washita Love Child," "Every Night Is Saturday Night," "You Bella Donna You," "Rock and Roll Gypsies," "Golden Sun Goddess," and "Crazy Love."
   Derek and the Dominos start recording their next album at Olympic Sound Studios, Barnes, London. Around thirteen tracks are recorded in various states of completion.

Above: Fairfield Halls, Croydon. (Barry Plummer)

Opposite page: Being interviewed by *Melody Maker*. (Barry Wentzell)

1971

MAY 1971

Derek and the Dominos break up after a disagreement during the recording of their second album at Olympic Sound Studios.

Eric spends the rest of the year at home having slowly become addicted to heroin.

JUNE 1971

Remember the Yardbirds LP released which contains a previously unreleased version of "I Wish You Would."

John Mayall releases his

Below: Eric deified. This slogan appeared on many walls throughout London during the late sixties. (Roger Perry)

Right: (Barry Wentzell)

Back to the Roots double album. Eric plays on "Prisons on the Road," "Accidental Suicide," "Home Again," "Looking at Tomorrow," "Force of Nature," and "Goodbye December."

JULY 1971

Buddy Guy and Junior Wells release *Play the Blues* LP. Eric plays on "A Man of Many Words," "My Baby She Left Me," "Come on in This House," "Have Mercy Baby," "T. Bone Shuffle," "A Poor Man's Plea," "Messin' With

the Kid," "I Don't Know," and "Bad Bad Whiskey."

Stephen Stills releases his *2* LP. Eric plays on "Fishes and Scorpions."

Bobby Whitlock releases his solo LP. Eric plays on "Where There's a Will There's a Way," "A Day Without Jesus," "Back in My Life Again," and "The Scenery Has Slowly Changed."

AUGUST 1971

Howlin' Wolf releases his *London Sessions* LP. Eric plays on "Rockin Daddy," "I Ain't Superstitious," "Sittin' on Top of the World," "Worried About My Baby," "What a Woman," "Poor Boy," "Built for Comfort," "Who's Been Talking," "Little Red Rooster," "Do the Do," "Highway 49," "Wang Dang Doodle."

1

Eric comes out of semiretirement to help out his friend George Harrison for a charity concert for the people of Bangla Desh.

The concert takes place at New York's Madison Square Garden. There are two shows, afternoon and evening. The band for this amazing show is: George Harrison (guitar, vocals), Eric Clapton (guitar), Jesse Davis (guitar), Leon Russell (piano), Ringo Starr (drums), Klaus Voormann (bass), Carl Radle (bass), Jim Keltner (drums), Billy Preston (organ), Badfinger (backing vocals), and Don Preston (guitar). Bob Dylan also appears.

The entire event is filmed and recorded for later release.

NOVEMBER 1971

Dr. John releases his *The Sun, Moon and Herbs* LP. Eric plays on "Back John the Conqueror," "Where Ya at Mule?," "Craney Crow," "Pots on Fiyo/Who I Got to Fall On," "Zu Zu Mandu," and "Familiar Reality."

1971/
1972/
1973

DECEMBER 1971
4

The Rainbow, London. Eric jams with Leon Russell.

Eric continues his semi-retirement. His record company releases various compilations to keep his name in the public eye.

JANUARY 1972

George Harrison's *Concert for Bangla Desh* triple LP released.

JUNE 1972

Cream *Live — Vol. 2* released.

JULY 1972

Bobby Keys releases his solo LP. Eric plays on "Steal From a King," "Bootleg," "Command Performance," and "Crispy Duck." "Layla" backed with "Bell Bottom Blues" released as a single. *History of Eric Clapton* double LP released.

AUGUST 1972

Music press announce that Eric is to top the bill at the Lincoln Festival with Stevie Wonder and, according to

All shots from the Concert for Bangla Desh, Madison Square Garden, New York, August 1, 1971. (Apple Records)

Robert Stigwood, the event is to be recorded. Needless to say, this never happens.

SEPTEMBER 1972

9

Eric flies out to see The Who in concert in Paris, after which he spends time with Keith Richards at his villa at Villefranche in the south of France.

John and Yoko release *Sometime in New York City*. Eric plays with a cast of thousands on one side of the "free" album.

OCTOBER 1972

Eric records with Stevie Wonder at Air Studios in London.

DECEMBER 1972

Bobby Whitlock releases his *Raw Velvet* LP. Eric plays on "Hello L.A., Bye Bye Birmingham" and "The Dreams of a Hobo."

Duane Allman: An Anthology released. This double LP features a hitherto unreleased track: Duane and Eric playing "Mean Old World." This LP, an essential purchase for guitar fans, is a showcase for Duane Allman's unique talent.

JANUARY 1973

13

The Rainbow Theatre, Lon-

don. Eric performs two shows, at 6:30 and 8:30, backed by Pete Townshend, Ronnie Wood, Stevie Winwood, Rebop, Jim Capaldi, Rick Grech, and Jimmy Karstein. Support is The Average White Band.

First show set: "Layla," "Badge," "Blues Power," "Nobody Knows You When You're Down and Out," "Roll It Over," "Why Does Love Got to Be So Sad," "Little Wing," "Bottle of Red Wine," "After Midnight," "Bell Bottom Blues," "Presence of the Lord," "Tell the Truth," "Pearly Queen," "Let It Rain," and "Crossroads."

Second show set: "Layla," "Badge," "Blues Power," "Nobody Knows You When You're Down and Out," "Roll It Over," "Why Does Love Got to Be So Sad," "Little Wing," "Bottle of Red Wine," "Presence Of the Lord," "Tell the Truth," "Pearly Queen," "Key to the Highway," "Let It

Rain," "Crossroads," and "Layla (reprise)."

Pete Townshend: It really wasn't difficult to get people to help. In fact you might be surprised at a few names I could mention who would have given their right arms to jam in this band.

Eric Clapton: I did that very much against my will. It was purely Townshend's idea. I'm indebted to him.

Eric plays a Fender Stratocaster for the first show and a Gibson Les Paul for the second. The shows are critically acclaimed in the press, but unfortunately when the live album of the event is released it does not evoke the atmosphere of the evening, mainly because it was recorded badly. Eric's comeback was a success and it was a shame that the album did not do justice to the event.

LIVE CREAM VOL 2

UK Polydor 2382119
US Atco SD 7005
Released July 1972

S i d e   O n e :
1. Deserted Cities of the Heart
2. White Room
3. Politician
4. Tales of Brave Ulysses

S i d e   T w o :
5. Sunshine of Your Love
6. Hideaway

1973/ 1974

Right: The comeback concert organized by Pete Townshend at London's Rainbow Theatre, January 13, 1973. (Barry Plummer)

HISTORY OF ERIC CLAPTON

UK Polydor 2659012
US Atco SD 2-803
Released July 1972

Side One:
1. I Ain't Got You
2. Hideaway
3. Tribute to Elmore
4. I Want to Know
5. Sunshine of Your Love
6. Crossroads
Side Two:
7. Sea of Joy
8. Only You Know and I Know
9. I Don't Want to Discuss It
10. Teasin'
11. Blues Power
Side Three:
12. Spoonful
13. Badge
Side Four:
14. Tell the Truth
15. Tell the Truth Jam
16. Layla

FEBRUARY 1973

Eric and Pete Townshend begin work on unreleased Derek and the Dominos material for possible release.

The rest of the year is spent at home with hardly any contact with the outside world. Although Eric had returned to the stage, he had not yet conquered his heroin addiction. It is later revealed that Eric worked part of the summer as a farm laborer in Wales.

MARCH 1973

Derek and the Dominos release a live double album *Live In Concert* recorded at the Fillmore East in New York on October 23, 1970.

APRIL 1973

Derek and the Dominos release a live single from their double album: "Why Does Love Got to Be So Sad" backed with "Presence of the Lord."

MAY 1973

Music From Free Creek double album released. Eric plays on "Road Song," "Getting Back to Molly," and "No One Knows."

SEPTEMBER 1973

Eric Clapton's *Rainbow Concert* LP is released.

FEBRUARY 1974

Eric attends Stevie Wonder concert at The Rainbow in London.

MARCH 1974

Eric records with The Who for their forthcoming movie of *Tommy* as well as taking part in the actual filming. He played the role of the preacher while miming to "Eyesight to the Blind."

APRIL 1974 10

Robert Stigwood throws a party at Soho's China Garden restaurant for Eric to celebrate his return to work.

Eric Clapton: I don't know why, but I just felt the time was right. I've been talking a lot to Robert about the best way of doing things. So what's happening is I'm going to Miami to record a new album. I'm going to America to form a new band as well. You remember Carl Radle? Well Carl is on bass and he's got a couple of guys together to play keyboards and drums, but I can't really say who they will be yet. It's all just starting to happen. But I want to record again, and I'll also be doing a tour of America and later on some dates in England. There's no name for the band yet, but I don't think it will be called Derek and the Dominos or anything like that. But basically I'm feeling very well. I'm really happy.

Guests at the party include Elton John, Pete Townshend, Rick Grech, Long John Baldry, and Ron Wood.

Far left: With Ron Wood at the Rainbow. (Barry Plummer)

Left: With Pete Townshend at the Rainbow. (Barry Wentzell)

Bottom: Flanked by Ron Wood and Pete Townshend at the Rainbow. (Chris Walter)

Eric Clapton's Rainbow Concert with Pete Townshend, Rick Grech, Jim Capaldi, Ronnie Wood, Rebop, Jimmy Karstein, Steve Winwood. Eric Clapton's Rainbow Concert with Pete Townshend Rick Grech, Jim Kar   od, Rebop, Jimmy Kar   Winwood. Eric Clapt   v Concert with Pete T   ck Grech, Jim Capald   od, Rebop, Jimmy Kar   Winwood. Eric Clapton's Rainbow Concert with Pete Townshend, Rick Grech, Jim Capaldi, Ronnie Wood, Rebop, Jimmy Karstein, Steve Winwood. Eric Clapton's Rainbow Concert with Pete Townshend, Rick Gre

RAINBOW CONCERT

UK RSO 2394116
US RSO 50877
Released September 1973

Side One:
1. Badge
2. Roll It Over
3. Presence of the Lord
Side Two:
4. Pearly Queen
5. After Midnight
6. Little Wing

1974

13

Eric flies to Miami and Criteria Recording Studios where his album will be produced by Tom Dowd.

The first few days are difficult with everyone trying to fit in and come up with ideas. However, as the month progressed, so did the music.

The initial idea was to use songs recorded during the aborted second Dominos album for side one, and side two would consist of new numbers which were about to be recorded. However, the sessions went so well that this idea was scrapped.

MAY 1974

By now Eric has his band together. Carl Radle calls in a couple of his musician friends from Tulsa, Jamie Oldaker (drums) and Dick Sims (keyboards). Yvonne Elliman, wife of Bill Oakes, an RSO executive, is often around the studio, and Eric decides that it would be good to have a female voice in the band to accompany him. Last, but certainly not least, comes George Terry on guitar. He is a local session guitarist that Eric had previously met during the "Layla" sessions.

They record around thirty

tracks. Sessions take place during the night, and during the day they relax in the sunshine at a house at 461 Ocean Boulevard.

JUNE 1974

In preparation for a massive tour, Eric Clapton and His Band, as they are to be known, rehearse in the Bahamas.

The Eric Clapton band opens with two warm-up shows in Scandinavia.

20

Tivoli Gardens, Stockholm

21

KB Halle, Copenhagen. Both

shows, although a little rough around the edges, are well received.

The band flies off to the States to begin their tour. The set differs every night. They normally open with two or three acoustic numbers before launching into their electric set. The selection comes from the following: "Smile," "Easy Now," "Let It Grow," "Can't Find My Way Home," which would be acoustic, followed by a selection from: "I Shot the Sheriff," "Willie and the Hand Jive," "Get Ready," "Presence of the Lord," "Steady Rollin'

Man," "Mainline Florida," "Have You Ever Loved a Woman," "Blues Power," "Can't Hold Out," "Let It Rain," "Tell the Truth," "Mean Old World," "Matchbox," "Badge," "Key to the Highway," "Little Wing," "Layla," "Crossroads," "Little Queenie."

28

Yale Bowl, New Haven

29

The Spectrum, Philadelphia

30

Nassau Coliseum, Uniondale, N.Y.

JULY 1974
2, 3

International Amphitheater, Chicago

4

Music Park, Columbus, Ohio

5

Three Rivers Stadium, Pittsburgh. The Band are supporting act on this show and, back at the hotel, Robbie Robertson celebrates his thirty-first birthday. He is not amused when Eric and Rick Danko attempt to cover him in birthday cake.

6

War Memorial Stadium, Buffalo. Eric jams with The Band on "Stage Fright."

Left: Copenhagen, June 21, 1974. (Jan Persson)

Bottom: Copenhagen. (Barry Wentzell)

21

Cow Palace, San Francisco. (2 shows—afternoon and evening).

23, 24

Coliseum, Denver

25

Keil Auditorium, St. Louis (2 shows—afternoon and evening)

27

Mississippi Valley Fairgrounds, Davenport, Miss.

28

Memorial Stadium, Memphis

29

Legion Field, Birmingham

31

City Park Stadium, New Orleans. "I Shot the Sheriff" backed with "Give Me Strength" released as Eric Clapton Band's first single.

AUGUST 1974

1

Omni, Atlanta. Pete Townshend jams with Eric on "Layla," "Baby Don't You Do It," and "Little Queenie" which also saw Keith Moon join in the proceedings.

2

Coliseum, Greensboro, N.C. Pete Townshend jams with Eric on "Willie and the Hand Jive," "Get Ready," "Layla," "Badge," "Little Queenie." Keith Moon jams for the last three numbers.

4

West Palm Beach International Raceway, Palm Beach. Keith Moon sings "Can't Explain." Pete Townshend and Joe Walsh also jam with Eric at various points in the concert.

5

Eric and his band go to Criteria Studios in Miami to record with Freddie King

Freddie King jams with Eric on "Have You Ever Loved a Woman" and "Hideaway."

7

Roosevelt Stadium, Jersey City, N.J. Freddie King jams with Eric on "Have You Ever Loved a Woman." After the concert Eric's limousine is mobbed by fans as quick getaway tactics break down.

9

The Forum, Montreal

10

Civic Center, Providence

12

Boston Garden, Boston

13

Madison Square Garden, New York. Todd Rundgren jams with Eric on "Little Queenie."

14

Capitol Center, Largo, Md.

18

Diablo Stadium, Tempe, Ariz.

19, 20

Long Beach Arena, Long Beach, Cal. John Mayall jams with Eric on a blues shuffle on 19.

1974

before heading off to Dynamic Sounds Studio in Kingston, Jamaica, to record new tracks for their next album.

Marcy Levy, a friend of the Tulsa Rhythm Section, joins the band to add more top harmonies.

Eric releases his new LP *461 Ocean Boulevard.*

Eric Clapton: **This album was very important to me because it was the first thing I'd done in three years and I only had, I think, maybe even only two songs to start it with, and like a snowball it gathered strength as it went along. Also it combined the strength of a new band that I didn't even know until we arrived together in the studio.**

461 OCEAN BOULEVARD

UK RSO 2479118
US RSO SO 4801
Released August 1974

Side One:
1. Motherless Children
2. Give Me Strength
3. Willie and the Hand Jive
4. Get Ready
5. I Shot the Sheriff

Side Two:
6. I Can't Hold Out Much Longer
7. Please Be With Me
8. Let It Grow
9. Steady Rollin' Man
10. Mainline Florida

SEPTEMBER 1974

Recording of the new album continues before a short tour of America followed by Japan and Europe. The set changes and Eric and His Band include some newly recorded songs. The set would consist of: "Smile," "Let It Grow," "Better Make It Through Today," "Can't Find My Way Home," "Let It Rain," "Little Wing," "Singin' The Blues," "I Shot the Sheriff," "Tell the Truth," "The Sky Is Crying," "Badge," "Little Rachel," "Willie and the Hand Jive," "Get Ready," "Blues Power," "Layla," "All I Have to Do Is Dream," "Steady Rollin' Man," and "Little Queenie."

The set varied every night; some songs were omitted and the running order often changed.

28
Hampton Roads Coliseum, Hampton Roads, Va.

29
Nassau Coliseum, Uniondale, N.Y. (2 shows 3:00 and 9:00)

30
Boston Garden, Boston

OCTOBER 1974
1
The Forum, Montreal

2
Maple Leaf Garden, Toronto

56

Top far left: U.S. tour, 1974. (Gijsbert Hanekroot)

Top and center near left: Nassau Coliseum. (David Redfern)

Bottom: Hammersmith Odeon, December 4, 1974. (Dezo Hoffman)

4, 5
Capitol Center, Largo, Md.

6
The Spectrum, Philadelphia. Eric and band go to Criteria Studios in Miami to complete work on their forthcoming album before embarking on their first ever tour of Japan.

Howlin' Wolf releases his *London Revisited* LP. Eric plays on "Going Down Slow," "The Killing Floor," and "I Want to Have a Word With You." (These were outtakes from the *London Sessions* LP.)

"Willie and the Hand Jive" backed with "Mainline Florida" released as their second single.

31
Budokan, Tokyo

NOVEMBER 1974
1, 2
Budokan, Tokyo

5, 6
Koseinenkin Hall, Osaka. After the Japanese tour everyone takes a well deserved break before their European tour.

26
Congress Centrum, Hamburg

27
Olympic Halle, Munich

1974/ 1975

28
Friedrich Ebert Halle, Ludwigshafen

29
Grugahalle, Essen

30
Ahoy Hall, Rotterdam. Freddie King releases his *Burglar* LP. Eric plays on "Sugar Sweet."

DECEMBER 1974

1
Palais Des Sports, Anvers

2
Parc Des Expositions, Paris

4, 5
Hammersmith Odeon, London. Ronnie Wood jams with Eric on "Steady Rollin' Man" and "Little Queenie" on 5.

JANUARY 1975
Eric records with Arthur Louis at Essex Sound Studios, London.

MARCH 1975
Eric and girlfriend Pattie Harrison attend London premiere of *Tommy* at the Leicester Square Theatre. Eric appears as the Preacher performing "Eyesight to the Blind."

APRIL 1975
Eric releases his *There's One in Every Crowd* album.

Eric Clapton: It's the kind of record that if you didn't like it after maybe the third or fourth time, you wouldn't play it again. But if you did like it and you carried on listening to it, you'd hear things that were really fine, just little things in the background, little touches.

Top right: Hammersmith Odeon, December 5, 1974. (Andre Csillag)

Center: Hammersmith Odeon. (Barry Wentzell)

Bottom far right and middle: Hammersmith Odeon. (Chris Walter)

Bottom near right: Hammersmith. (LFI)

Left: Madison Square
Garden, New York, July 13,
1974. (Stephen Morley)

59

1975

"Swing Low, Sweet Chariot" backed with "Pretty Blue Eyes" released as their third single.

Eric becomes a tax exile and his new base is a luxury villa in the Bahamas. He is only allowed sixty days a year to visit England, and even then he is not allowed to perform live!

The set for the Australian tour would be taken from the following: "Badge," "Steady Rollin' Man," "Key to the Highway," "Milk Cow Blues," "Can't Find My Way Home," "Teach Me to Be Your Woman," "Nobody Knows You When You're Down and Out," "I Shot the Sheriff," "Layla," "Little Wing," "Tell the Truth," "Let It Grow."

7, 8
HIC Arena, Honolulu

10, 11
Western Springs, Auckland, New Zealand. Eric plays to 18,000 people.

13, 14, 15, 16
Festival Hall, Brisbane, Australia

17
Hordern Pavilion, Sydney

18
Concert Hall, Perth

19, 20, 21
Hordern Pavilion, Sydney

22
Theatre Centre, Canberra, Australia

23, 24
Festival Hall, Brisbane

26
Memorial Park Drive, Adelaide

28
Entertainment Center, Perth

MAY 1975

On his return to England, Eric has a near fatal accident when his Ferrari collides with a large truck on a country lane near his home. Luckily, the car is the only thing that is badly damaged. A picture of it is to be found on the inside of the *Slowhand* album.

JUNE 1975

Prime Cuts (10-inch maxi sampler) is released this month. It features a live version of "Smile" recorded at the Long Beach Arena on July 20, 1974.

Start of massive U.S. tour which will last until August 30 with a small break midway.

The set varies every night and is taken from the following: "Layla," "Bell Bottom Blues," "Key to the Highway," "Mainline Florida," "Keep on Growing," "Can't Find My Way Home," "Carnival,"

THERE'S ONE IN EVERY CROWD

UK RSO 2479132
US RSO SO 4806
Released April 1975

Side One:
1. We've Been Told (Jesus Coming Soon)
2. Swing Low Sweet Chariot
3. Little Rachel
4. Don't Blame Me
5. The Sky Is Crying

Side Two:
6. Singin' the Blues
7. Better Make It Through Today
8. Pretty Blue Eyes
9. High
10. Opposites

"Stormy Monday," "Little
Wing," "Tell the Truth," "Why
Does Love Got to Be So Sad,"
"Sunshine of Your Love,"
"Motherless Children," "Mean
Old World," "Driftin' Blues,"
"Teach Me to Be Your
Woman," "Badge," "Let It
Rain," "Blues Power,"
"Knockin' on Heaven's Door,"
"Further on Up the Road,"
"Crossroads," "I Shot the
Sheriff," "Better Make It
Through Today," and
"Eyesight to the Blind." As
Santana was the support band
on most of the tour, Carlos
Santana would normally end
up jamming on the encores.

14
Tampa Stadium, Tampa, Fla.

15
Coliseum, Jacksonville

16
Criteria Studios, Miami. Eric
and His Band record their
version of "Knockin' on
Heaven's Door."

1975

17
Mobile Municipal Auditorium, Mobile

18
Mid-South Coliseum, Memphis

19
Coliseum, Knoxville

20
Coliseum, Charlotte, N.C.

21
Cincinnati Gardens, Cincinnati

22
Madison Square Garden, New York. Eric jams with the Rolling Stones on their encore of "Sympathy for the Devil."

Over the next few days Eric and His Band record some new songs for possible release at Electric Lady Studios in New York. One, "Carnival," was previewed on the tour, and featured the Rolling Stones along with all of Eric's band. They recorded around ten takes, but due to contractual difficulties, it remains unreleased.

23
Niagara Convention Center, Niagara Falls

24
Civic Center, Springfield, Mass.

25
Civic Center, Providence. Eric performs "Sunshine of Your Love" for the first time since Cream disbanded.

26
Performing Arts Center, Saratoga, N.Y.

28
Nassau Coliseum, Uniondale, N.Y. (Live recording) Carlos Santana, John McLaughlin, and Alphonze Mouzon jam with Eric on versions of "Stormy Monday" and "Eyesight to the Blind."

"Further on Up the Road" from the album *EC Was Here* is taken from this gig.

29
Civic Center, New Haven

30
Civic Center, Pittsburgh

JULY 1975

Tommy soundtrack album is released in July. Eric plays on "Eyesight to the Blind" and "Sally Simpson."

1
Olympia Stadium, Detroit

3
Baltimore Stadium, Baltimore

4
Coliseum, Cleveland

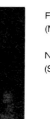

15

Swing Auditorium, San Bernardino. Jerry McGee jams with Eric on "Further on Up the Road" and "Stormy Monday."

16

Sports Arena, San Diego

17

Community Center, Tucson

18

Civic Center, El Paso

20

Sam Houston Coliseum, Houston

21

Tarrant County Convention Center, Fort Worth

22

Myriad Coliseum, Oklahoma City

23

Assembly Center, Tulsa

24

Hirsch Coliseum, Shreveport

27

Market Square Arena, Indianapolis

28

Municipal Auditorium, Charleston, West Va.

29

Coliseum, Greensboro, S.C.

30

The Scope, Norfolk. Poco jams with Eric on "Let It Rain."

Eric Clapton: **You won't catch me saying this is my best band. The last time I said that The Dominos broke up a month later. But I'd go see us.**

EC WAS HERE

UK RSO 2394160
US RSO SO 4809
Released August 1975

Side One:
1. Have You Ever Loved a Woman
2. Presence of the Lord
3. Drifting Blues
Side Two:
4. Can't Find My Way Home
5. Ramblin' on My Mind
6. Further on Up the Road

5

Chicago Stadium, Chicago

7

Met Sports Center, Minneapolis

8

Dane County Coliseum, Madison, Wisc.

10

Kansas Municipal Auditorium, Kansas City, Mo.

11

Kiel Auditorium, St. Louis, Mo.

28

Columbia Studios, New York. Eric joins Bob Dylan to record numbers for Bob's upcoming album. At least seven numbers are recorded. In Dylan's usual manner, only one number was released from this session. All the others were either scrapped or rerecorded.

AUGUST 1975

3

P&E Coliseum, Vancouver, B.C.

4

Coliseum, Portland, Oregon

5

Coliseum, Seattle

6

Coliseum, Spokane

9

Stanford University, Stanford, Cal.

11

Salt Palace, Salt Lake City

12

Denver Coliseum, Denver

14

The Forum, Los Angeles. Keith Moon, Carlos Santana, and Joe Cocker join Eric on stage at various times throughout the show.

1975/ 1976

NO REASON TO CRY

UK RSO 2394160
US RSO 1-3004
Released August 1976

Side One:
1. Beautiful Thing
2. Carnival
3. Sign Language
4. County Jail Blues
5. All Our Pasttimes

Side Two:
6. Hello Old Friend
7. Double Trouble
8. Innocent Times
9. Hungry
10. Black Summer

Center right: Pavilion, Hemel Hempstead, July 29, 1976. (Andre Csillag)

Right: All shots from Crystal Palace Bowl concert, London, July 31, 1976. (Barry Plummer)

"Knockin' on Heaven's Door" backed with "Someone Like You" released as a single by Eric.

"Knockin' on Heaven's Door" backed with "Plum" released by Arthur Louis. Eric plays on both tracks.

Arthur Louis releases his *First Album* in Japan only. Eric plays on "Knockin' on Heaven's Door," "Plum," "The Dealer," "Still It Feels Good," "Come on and Love Me," "Train 444," "Go and Make It Happen."

SEPTEMBER 1975

Eric returns to England for a short vacation in the U.K.

11

Hammersmith Odeon, London. Santana plays the Odeon and brings on Eric for the encore. Unfortunately, he couldn't even jam as he was still a tax exile.

14

Eric appears as a clown for the Central Remedial Clinic and Variety Club of Ireland at Straffan House, home of film producer Kevin McClory for a charity show alongside Shirley MacLaine, Judy Geeson, Sean Connery, and Burgess Meredith, with music supplied by The Chieftains. A thirty-seven-minute film of the event is released, called *Circasia*.

Eric stays in Ireland for a break in County Kildare.

Eric releases his live album *EC Was Here*.

Eric Clapton: **There was a long battle about this album and I refused to let it go out until I heard . . . I think it was "Have You Ever Loved a Woman" and it was played to me by Tom Dowd in the studio in Criteria, and he just said, "Listen to this," and the rest of it was built round that for me. He convinced me with that one track that it was worth doing a live album and he had complete control over what went on there.**

Toward the end of September

Eric heads off to New York for some recording before starting a Japanese tour.

OCTOBER 1975

The Japanese set is virtually the same as U.S.A '75.

22, 23
Festival Hall, Osaka

24
Kyoto Kaikan Hall, Kyoto

26
Sunpan Kaikan, Shizuoka

27
Kitu-Kyushu Shi Ritsu Sogo Taiiku-Kan, Kokura

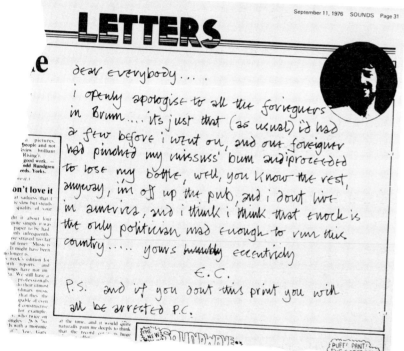

LETTERS

September 11, 1976 SOUNDS Page 31

dear everybody....

i openly apologise to all the foreigners in Brum.... its just that (as usual) i'd had a few before i went on, and our foreigner had pinched my missus' bum and proceeded to lose my bottle, well, you know the rest, anyway, im off up the pub, and i don't live in america, and i think i think that enoch is the only politician mad enough to run this country..... yours humbly eccentricly

E.C.

P.S. and if you don't this print you will all be arrested P.C.

29

Shizuoka Sumpu Kaikan, Shizuoka

NOVEMBER 1975

Dr. John releases his *Hollywood Be Thy Name* LP. Eric plays congas at the session but it is hard to say for certain which tracks he is on.

1, 2

Budokan, Tokyo

After the Japanese tour, Eric returns to America to record and produce a duo called Tom and Don, but nothing is ever released.

JANUARY 1976

Bob Dylan releases his *Desire* album. Eric plays on "Romance in Durango."

FEBRUARY–APRIL 1976

The early part of the year is spent at The Band's Shangri-La Studio for the recording of "No Reason to Cry." Many guests drop by the studio for various jams and guest spots: Bob Dylan, Ronnie Wood, Robbie Robertson (who contributes some stunning lead guitar work on the Dylan track "Sign Language"), Rick Danko, Levon Helm, Garth

Hudson, and Richard Manuel, to name but a few.

Eric Clapton: I think my best stuff has been done in American studios. Shangri-La was the finest studio of all to work in. We cut something like twenty-five tracks in three weeks out of nowhere, out of the blue. It was just like falling rain, and the outtakes ... whoever's got them is sitting on a mint, because they're beautiful. Some of the best stuff didn't get on the album ... like instrumentals.

I had a magnificent birthday party right in the middle of the sessions and we decided to record everything and everybody that came into the studio. There's Billy [Preston] singing a couple of Ray Charles songs with The Band backing him along with Jesse Ed Davis, me, Robbie [Robertson] and Woody (Ron Wood) on guitars. Bob [Dylan] showed up about eight o'clock in the morning and it went on from there.

During this period Eric also jammed with The Crusaders at the Roxy in Los Angeles along with Stevie Wonder, Elton John, and Rick Danko. He also took part in a session for a Van Morrison album which remains unreleased.

MAY 1976
15

Granby Halls, Leicester. Jams with the Rolling Stones on "Brown Sugar" and "Key to the Highway."

1976

JUNE 1976

Joe Cocker releases his *Stingray* album. Eric plays on "Worrier."

JULY 1976

29

British Tour opens at the Pavilion, Hemel Hempstead. The show opens with two acoustic numbers: "Hello Old Friend" and "All Our Past Times." The remainder of the set varies each night but would be taken from the following: "I Shot the Sheriff," "Nobody Knows You When You're Down and Out," "Can't Find My Way Home," "Tell the Truth," "Kansas City," "Innocent Times," "Stormy Monday," "Going Down Slow," "Double Trouble," "Blues Power," "Layla," "Key to the Highway," "Knockin' on Heaven's Door," and "Further on Up the Road."

The band consists of Eric Clapton (guitar, vocals), George Terry (guitar, vocals), Carl Radle (bass), Dick Sims (keyboards), Jamie Oldaker (drums), Sergio Pastora Rodriguez (percussion), Marcy Levy (vocals), Yvonne Elliman (vocals).

31

Crystal Palace Bowl, London. This was the ninth Garden Party at the Bowl and support artists were Freddie King, the Jess Roden Band, Barbara Dixon, Dick and the Firemen, and The Chieftains.

Larry Coryell jams with Eric on "Going Down Slow" and "Stormy Monday" as well as the encore of "Further on Up the Road," joined by Freddie King and Ronnie Wood.

AUGUST 1976

1

Gaumont, Southampton

2

Town Hall, Torquay

Top right: With Pattie designing album covers. (Graham Wiltshire)

Bottom right: Crystal Palace. (Andre Csillag)

Top and bottom left:
Crystal Palace. (Relay
Photos)

3

ABC Theatre, Plymouth

5

Odeon, Birmingham. Van Morrison joins Eric for "Kansas City" and a few blues numbers. This is the gig where Eric makes his controversial political speech, apparently in support of Enoch Powell.

Eric Clapton: **I just don't know what came over me that night. It must have been something that happened in the day but it came out in this garbled thing. I'm glad you printed the letter though.**

The letter Eric refers to is the one he sent to *Sounds* (issue September 11, 1976) after hostile press over-reaction. In it he gave the reasons for his behavior.

6

Belle Vue King's Hall, Manchester. Van Morrison again joins Eric for "Kansas City" and a few blues numbers.

7

University, Lancaster

9, 10

Apollo, Glasgow

12

City Hall, Newcastle-upon-Tyne

13

Spa Pavilion, Bridlington

15

ABC Theatre, Blackpool. Eric and His Band sing "Happy Birthday" to Roger Forrester, his manager, during their set.

17

Warner Holiday Camp, Hayling Island. Eric plays to impartial holidaymakers numbering under one thousand. No members of the public are allowed in.

1976

Promoter *Harvey Goldsmith:* I haven't heard him play like this the whole tour.

Eric Clapton: I'm always more comfortable in situations like that. The pressures are off and I feel comfortable because there is no one to prove myself to.

SEPTEMBER 1976

7

Eric and Pattie Harrison attend Buddy Holly's fortieth birthday anniversary party in the company of Paul and Linda McCartney, Elton John, Phil Manzanera, Andy Mackay, Stephen Bishop, Steve Harley, and Eric Stewart, to name but a few. Norman Petty, Buddy Holly's producer and cowriter, is guest of honor.

Eric writes "Wonderful Tonight" after the party.

Eric Clapton: The songs you write very quickly are always the best . . . the ones that are written in the space of a day. It was just about taking the old woman out and getting too sloshed to drive home.

17

Eric and Pattie attend Croydon's Fairfield Hall for the start of Don Williams' British tour.

Eric invites everyone back to his house for a jam session which lasts well into the early hours.

Top right: With Pattie and Stephen Bishop, December, 1976. (Alan Messer)

Center and bottom right: At Cranleigh Village Hall, February 14, 1977.

Below: Robbie Robertson and Rick Danko of The Band with Ronnie Hawkins at *The Last Waltz* concert, San Francisco, November 26, 1976. (United Artists)

THE BAND **THE LAST WALTZ** United Artists

18

Eric joins Don Williams at Hammersmith Odeon in London to play some of the finest dobro you're likely to hear. Eric also introduces Pete Townshend and Ronnie Lane to Williams backstage.

Don Williams: He's an incredible picker. Eric plays a lot of rhythms and stuff that are very close to the way I feel and some of the songs he's written are just . . . really fine. He's phenomenal.

Ringo Starr releases his *Rotogravure* LP. Eric wrote and plays on "This Be Called a Song."

NOVEMBER 1976

5

Short U.S. tour opens at the Bayfront Center in St. Petersburg, Fla. Same band as British tour.

Shows open with two acoustic numbers, "Hello Old Friend" and "Sign Language." The remainder of the set varies each night but is taken from the following: "Tell the Truth," "Double Trouble," "Blues Power," "Knockin' on Heaven's Door," "Can't Find My Way Home," "Key to the Highway," "I Shot the Sheriff," "One Night," "Layla," "Further on Up the Road," "Badge," and "Have You Ever Loved a Woman."

6

Sportatorium, Miami

7

Coliseum, Jacksonville

9

Omni, Atlanta

10

Municipal Auditorium, Mobile

11

LSU Assembly Center, Baton Rouge

13

Hofeinz Pavilion, Houston

14

Convention Center, Dallas. Freddie King joins Eric on "Further on Up the Road." The majority of the show is broadcast at a later date.

15

Memorial Auditorium, Dallas. Eric joins Texas Blues Jam playing alongside Bugs Henderson, Freddie King, Bobby Chitwood, and Ron Thompson.

16

Lloyd Noble Center, Norman, Okla.

18

Pan Am Center, Las Cruces, N.M.

19

Coliseum, Phoenix

20

Sports Arena, San Diego

22

The Forum, Los Angeles

26

Winterland, San Francisco. Eric joins a cast of thousands for The Band's farewell con-
cert. Eric plays "Further on Up the Road" and "All Our Pastimes" backed by The Band. He returns to join Van Morrison, Ron Wood, Bob Dylan, Neil Young, Joni Mitchell, Ronnie Hawkins, Dr. John, Neil Diamond, Paul Butterfield, Bobby Charles, Ringo Starr and, of course, The Band, for a rendition of "I Shall Be Released." Finally, Eric, along with Steve Stills, Carl Radle, Ronnie Wood, Neil Young, Robbie Robertson, Levon Helm, Ringo Starr, Paul Butterfield, and Dr. John return to the stage for a couple of instrumental jams.

A large amount of the concert is released both on album and video as *The Last Waltz*. The highlight is Muddy Waters' amazing version of "Mannish Boy."

Eric also finds time to jam with Freddie King at the Starwood in Los Angeles along with Bonnie Bramlett.

DECEMBER 1976

Stephen Bishop releases his first solo album *Careless*. Eric plays on "Sinking in an Ocean of Tears" and "Save It for a Rainy Day."

1977

Right: Hammersmith
Odeon, April 27, 1977.
(Barry Plummer)

FEBRUARY 1977
14

Eric plays an unpublicized St. Valentine's Day dance at Cranleigh Village Hall in Surrey.

The concert posters advertise the group as Eddie and the Earth Tremors, although it is common knowledge locally who is appearing. The evening is arranged by the local Round Table charity. As Eric takes a keen interest in local affairs, he is only too happy to play for nothing as long as his name is not mentioned. As a result Cranleigh Cottage Hospital benefits by £1,000.

Backed by Ronnie Lane (guitar and vocals), Bruce Rowland (drums), Charlie Hart (accordion, violin, keyboards), and Brian Belshaw (bass), this one-off band performs such songs as "How Come," "Willie and the Hand Jive," "Oo La La," "Goodnight Irene," and "Alberta, Alberta." A good time is had by all.

Kinky Friedman releases his *Lasso From El Paso* LP Eric plays on "Kinky" and "Ol' Ben Lucas."

February also sees the release of "Carnival" backed with "Hungry" as a single.

APRIL 1977

Eric and his band spend a few days at Pinewood Studios rehearsing for their upcoming British tour. Shows open with acoustic versions of "Hello Old Friend," "Sign Language," and "Alberta, Alberta." An electric set follows which is taken from the following: "Tell the Truth," "Knockin' On Heaven's Door," "Steady Rollin' Man," "Can't Find My Way Home," "Further On Up the Road," "Stormy Monday," "Badge," "Nobody Knows You When You're Down and Out," "I Shot the Sheriff," "Double Trouble," "Key to the Highway," "All Our Pastimes," "Crossroads," "Layla," and "Willie and the Hand Jive."

20

British tour opens at the De Montfort Hall, Leicester.

21

Belle Vue, Manchester

22

Victoria Hall, Stoke on Trent

23

Apollo Center, Glasgow

24

City Hall, Newcastle-upon-Tyne

26

BBC-TV Theatre, Shepherds Bush, London.
Eric and His Band are filmed for *The Old Grey Whistle Test* TV program.

27, 28

Hammersmith Odeon, London. On 28, Ronnie Lane and Patti Boyd join Eric for "Willie and the Hand Jive." Rose Clapp, Eric's grandmother, also runs across the stage to give Eric a hug after the encore.

29

Rainbow Theatre, London. Pete Townshend jams with Eric on "Layla" and "Crossroads."

MAY 1977

Eric and His Band enter Olympic Studios in Barnes for the recording of "Slowhand" with Glyn Johns producing. Mel Collins on sax guests on "The Core."

Eric Clapton: "Slowhand" for me is a very nervous sung album, especially after "No Reason to Cry." Maybe it was because of the lack of material we had when we went in to cut it or the difference in surroundings. Anyway, for me the best track has got to be "Wonderful Tonight" because the song is nice. It was written about my sweetheart, and whether or not it was recorded well or I played it well doesn't make any difference, because the song is still nice.

Corky Laing releases his *Makin' It on the Street* album. Eric plays on "On My Way."
   Roger Daltrey releases his *One of The Boys* LP. Eric is credited.

JUNE 1977

Eric and His Band start a short Irish and European tour.

4, 6

National Stadium, Dublin

7

The Old Grey Whistle Test broadcast in U.K.

9

Falkoner Theatre, Copenhagen

10

Stadthalle, Bremen

11

Groenoordhalle, Leiden

13

Forest National, Brussels

14

Le Pavilion, Paris. Ringo Starr on tambourine joins Eric for "Badge."

15

Philipshalle, Dusseldorf

17

Rhein-Neckar-Halle, Heidelberg

19

Mehrzweckhalle, Wetzikon

20

Olympic Halle, Munich. For this European tour Eric hires the dining car from the Orient Express, one elegant day coach, and one sleeper car from Denmark.

Eric Clapton: It is the only way to travel. I'm amazed how well it's worked. I really thought that we'd wake up one morning and find ourselves hundreds of miles away on the wrong side of Europe. Now I don't want to travel any other way.

JULY 1977

Eric and Pattie take a short holiday on board Robert Stigwood's yacht *The Welsh Liberty* which takes them from Nice to Ibiza for a short tour.

AUGUST 1977
5

The Bull Ring, Ibiza

11

Nouveau Pabellon Club, Barcelona

Eric Clapton: In Ibiza, when

Left: Hammersmith Odeon, April 28, 1977. (Relay Photos)

1977

you walked into the dressing room, there was the operating table with blood gutters down the side of it for the matadors, when they get patched up. It was all a bit grim. I thought it was going to be a lovely old building like a rodeo place and it turned out to be a concrete monstrosity in the middle of nowhere.

SEPTEMBER 1977

Start of short Japanese tour. The band is basically the same as the European tour except that Sergio Pastora

release *Rough Mix* LP. Eric plays on "Rough Mix," "Annie," "April Fool," and "Till the Rivers All Run Dry."

Rodriguez and Yvonne Elliman had now left.

The set is taken from the following: "The Core," "Badge," "Double Trouble," "Knockin' on Heaven's Door," "Bottle of Red Wine," "Nobody Knows You When You're Down and Out," "Alberta, Alberta," "We're All the Way," "Sign Language," "Tell the Truth," "Stormy Monday," "Layla," and "Key to the Highway."

26
Festival Hall, Osaka

27
Ken Taiiku-Kan, Yokohama

28, 29
Kaikan Hall, Kyoto

30
Shi Kokaido, Nagoya. Pete Townshend and Ronnie Lane

SLOWHAND

UK RSO 2479201
US RSO RS 1-3030
Released November 1977

Side One:
1. Cocaine
2. Wonderful Tonight
3. Lay Down Sally
4. We're All the Way

Side Two:
5. The Core
6. May You Never
7. Mean Old Frisco
8. Peaches and Diesel

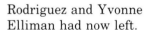

OCTOBER 1977

1
Festival Hall, Osaka

2
Japan

3
Japan

4
Makima-Nailce Arena, Sapporo

6, 7
Budokan, Tokyo

9, 10
HIC Arena, Honolulu.
Freddie King album *1934–1976* is released. Eric plays on "Sugar Sweet," "TV Mama," "Gambling Woman Blues," and "Further on Up the Road."

1977/
1978

Top: U.S. tour, 1978.
(Michael Putland)

Bottom far right:
Hammersmith Odeon,
December 1978. (Barry
Plummer)

Bottom near right: U.S.
tour, 1978. (Neal Preston)

NOVEMBER 1977

"Lay Down Sally" backed with "Cocaine" released as a single.
  Eric releases his new album *Slowhand*.

JANUARY 1978

Rick Danko releases his solo LP. Eric plays on "New Mexico."

FEBRUARY 1978

1

North American tour opens at the PNE Coliseum, Vancouver. As always the set would vary from night to night but would be taken from the following: "Peaches and Diesel," "Wonderful Tonight," "Lay Down Sally," "Next Time You See Her," "The Core," "All the Way," "Rodeo Man," "Fools Paradise," "Cocaine," "Badge," "Let It Rain," "Knockin' on Heaven's Door," "Key to the Highway," "Going Down Slow," "Layla," "Bottle of Red Wine," "You'll Never Walk Alone."
  The band consists of Eric Clapton (guitar, vocals), George Terry (guitar, vocals), Carl Radle (bass), Dick Sims (keyboards), Jamie Oldaker (drums), and Marcy Levy (vocals).

3

Exhibition Coliseum, Edmonton

5

Paramount Theater, Seattle

6

WSU Coliseum, Pullman, Wash.

8

Paramount Theater, Portland

10

Coliseum, Oakland, Cal.

11, 12

Civic Auditorium, Santa Monica

13

Aladdin Theater, Las Vegas

15

McNichols Arena, Denver

18

Metropolitan Center, Minneapolis

19

University of Iowa Hilton Coliseum, Ames, Iowa

20

Convention Center, Kansas City, Kan.

21

Keil Auditorium, St. Louis

23

Stadium, Chicago

24

Gardens, Louisville

26

Civic Center Arena, Huntington, Ind.

28

Municipal Auditorium, Nashville. Don Williams opens this show for Eric with a great thirty-minute set including such songs as "I Recall a Gypsy Woman" and "Shelter of Your Eyes."

Don Williams: It was tough, but I expected it to be an uphill fight. Eric and I really want to work together more because we appreciate each other's music so much. Hopefully we'll get to try it out some other places and maybe approach it a little differently.

MARCH 1978

"Wonderful Tonight" backed with "Peaches and Diesel" released as a single.

1

Mid-South Coliseum, Memphis

2

Boutwell Auditorium, Birmingham

3

For a breather from the tour, Eric returns to the U.K. deciding to play small venues.

Eric Clapton: It's a deliberate move. I don't play the huge stadiums now, because I want to get closer to the audiences. Until now they've never seen me at my best in America. I can't wait to get back there.

11

Attends West Bromwich Albion v. Nottingham Forest match. W.B.A.—whom Eric supports—wins.

17

Returns to U.S. for continuation of tour.

19

Jai-Alai Frontun, Miami

20

Civic Center Coliseum, Lakeland, Fla.

21

Civic Center, Savannah

22

Coliseum, Macon

24

Memorial Coliseum, Charlotte, Va.

25

Carolina Coliseum, Columbia, S.C.

26

Von Braun Civic Center, Huntsville. King Biscuit Flour Hour broadcasts ninety minutes of Eric's Santa Monica show from February 11.

28

Cobo Hall, Detroit

29

Convention Center, Cleveland

31

Civic Center Arena, Baltimore

Left: Eric and Don Williams, 1978. (Richard Young)

Center: With Bob Dylan, Blackbushe, July 15, 1978.

1978

APRIL 1978

1

The Spectrum, Philadelphia

2, 3

Radio City Music Hall, New York

5

Civic Center, Springfield, Mass.

7

The Forum, Montreal

9

Maple Leaf Gardens, Toronto

19

Pinewood Studios. Eric takes part in Alexis Korner's fiftieth birthday party celebration. This show will later be available on video and record.

Eric and band take a well deserved holiday and prepare themselves for a series of festival appearances as support for Bob Dylan.

I Jah Man releases his *Haile I Hymn* album. Eric was at the sessions along with Stevie Winwood.

The Band's *Last Waltz* LP is released. Eric plays on "Further on Up the Road" and "I Shall Be Released."

JUNE 1978

23

Feijenoord Stadium, Rotterdam. This is the first of three dates supporting Bob Dylan.

June also sees the release of the *White Mansions* LP. Eric plays on "White Trash" and "Kentucky Racehorse."

JULY 1978

1

Zeppelinfield, Nuremburg. After his own set, Eric joins Bob Dylan for "I'll Be Your Baby Tonight," and "The Times They Are A-Changin'."

7, 8

National Stadium, Dublin. These two dates are used as a warm-up for their forthcoming

show at the huge Blackbushe Festival.

15

Blackbushe Aerodrome, Hampshire. 200,000 people attend the last date of Bob Dylan's European tour. Support acts are Merger, Lake, Graham Parker, Eric Clapton, and Joan Armatrading.

£1.27 million is the staggering amount of gate money, £350,000 going to Bob Dylan.

Eric joins Dylan for a rousing guitar solo on "Forever Young."

AUGUST–SEPTEMBER 1978

Eric and band enter Olympic Studios in Barnes to record "Backless" with Glyn Johns producing.

Bob Dylan gives Eric two unreleased songs to record, "Walk Out in the Rain" and "If I Don't Be There by Morning."

Benny Gallagher and Graham Lyle guest on "Golden Ring."

Eric Clapton: **The title came from the Dylan gig we did at Blackbushe, where it became very apparent that he knew exactly what was going on around him all the time. So it's a tribute to Bob, really. I mean . . . if you were backstage, he expected you to be putting as much into it as he was. You couldn't just stand there and be one of the roadies, you had to actually focus all your attention on him, and if you didn't, he knew it, and he'd turn around and he'd look at you and you'd get daggers.**

The best things that happened on "Backless" were the things that happened at the time. I got away with one song, "Golden Ring," which I think is the strongest song on the album, because I wrote it because I was fed up with the general sort of apathy of everyone involved, and I just thought, "Well, I'll take a song in there and whether they like it or not, we'll do it—they'll learn it and record it and we'll put it on the record, and that's that." And that kind of conviction carried the thing through.

"Promises" backed with "Watch Out for Lucy" released as a single.

OCTOBER 1978

Eric and band, which now consists only of Jamie Oldaker, Carl Radle, and Dick Sims, rehearse for the forthcoming European tour.

As usual the sets vary each night and are to be taken from the following: "Golden Ring," "Someone Like You" (B-side of "Knockin' on Heaven's Door"), "Loving You," "Layla," "Worried Life Blues," "Tulsa Time," "Early in the Morning," "I'll Make Love to You Anytime," "Double Trouble," "Badge," "Wonderful Tonight," "If I Don't Be There by Morning," "Key to the Highway," "Cocaine," "Crossroads," and "Further on Up the Road."

Muddy Waters is the support act for the tour and he would often jam during Eric's encore.

NOVEMBER 1978

5

Pabellon Deportivo Del Real Madrid, Madrid

6

Club Juventus, Barcelona

8

Palais Des Sports, Lyon

10

Saarlandhalle, Saarbrucken

11

Festhalle, Frankfurt

12

Olympic Halle, Munich

14

Philipshalle, Dusseldorf

15, 16

Congresscentrum, Hamburg

18

Le Pavilion, Paris

19

Forest National, Brussels

20

Jaap Edenhal, Amsterdam

24

Apollo Theatre, Glasgow. Eric plays Robert Johnson's "Kindhearted Woman Blues." Lucky Scots.

25

City Hall, Newcastle-upon-Tyne

26

Apollo Theatre, Manchester

28

Victoria Hall, Hanley

1978/ 1979

Top right: Wedding photograph, March 27, 1979, Tucson, Arizona.

BACKLESS

UK RSO 5001
US RSO RS 1-3039
Released November 1978

Side One:
1. Walk Out in the Rain
2. Watch Out for Lucy
3. I'll Make Love to You
4. Roll It
5. Tell Me That You Love Me

Side Two:
6. If I Don't Be There by Morning
7. Early in the Morning
8. Promises
9. Golden Ring
10. Tulsa Time

29

Gala Ballroom, West Bromwich

DECEMBER 1978

1

Gaumont Theatre, Southampton

2

Conference Centre, Brighton

5, 6

Hammersmith Odeon, London. Muddy Waters joins Eric for the encore.

7

Civic Hall, Guildford. Muddy Waters joins Eric for "Hey Baby." George Harrison and Elton John join Eric for "Further on Up the Road."

Eric's new album *Backless* released.

FEBRUARY 1979

"If I Don't Be There by Morning" backed with "Tulsa Time" released as Eric's new single.

George Harrison releases his *George Harrison* LP. Eric plays on "Love Comes to Everyone."

MARCH 1979

Eric prepares for Irish and American tours. The band now consists of Eric (guitar, vocals), Albert Lee (guitar, vocals), Dick Sims (organ), Carl Radle (bass), and Jamie Oldaker (drums).

The set for the Irish tour would normally run as follows: "Loving You Is Sweeter Than Ever," "Worried Life Blues," "Badge," "Wonderful Tonight," "Crossroads," "If I Don't Be There by Morning," "Double Trouble," "Tulsa Time," "Early in the Morning," "Cocaine," "Key to the Highway," "Carnival," "Layla," and "Further On Up the Road."

8

City Hall, Cork

9

St. John Lyn's, Tralee

11

Leisureland, Galway

12

Savoy Theatre, Limerick

13

Stand Hill, Sligo

15

Downtown Club, Dundalk

16

Army Drill Hall, Dublin. (This gig was done as a thank you to the army for helping Eric ship his gear on previous tours.)

17

National Stadium, Dublin.

Eric and his new band hire a hall at Ascot race course for rehearsals for their huge upcoming U.S. tour.

Eric Clapton: **Roger Forrester said to me that certain production type songs like "Layla" or "Badge" were songs where it definitely needed a fuller sound, and suggested Albert Lee. And it was just like bang — light bulb — and I thought, why didn't I think of that?**

The set list for the U.S. tour would normally run as follows: "Badge," "If I Don't Be There by Morning," "Worried Life Blues," "Crossroads," "Knockin' on Heaven's Door," "Tulsa Time," "Early in the Morning," "Watch Out for Lucy," "Setting Me Up," "Double Trouble," "Lay Down Sally," "Wonderful Tonight," "Cocaine," "Layla," and "Further On Up the Road."

27

Eric marries Pattie in Tucson, Arizona, before starting his American tour. Muddy Waters is the support act.

28

Community Center, Tucson. During "Wonderful Tonight" Eric brings his bride on stage and dedicates the song to her.

29

Civic Center, Albuquerque

31

University of Texas Special Events Center, El Paso

APRIL 1979

1

Chaparral Center, Midland, Texas

3

Lloyd Noble Center, Norman, Okla.

4

Hammons Center, Springfield, Mo.

6

Assembly Center, Tulsa

Top: In Poland, 1979. (Chris Horler)

Bottom: A restless audience in Poland, 1979. (Chris Horler)

79

1979

7
Convention Center, Pine Bluff, Ark.

9
Summit, Houston

10
Tarrant County Convention Center, Fort Worth

11
Municipal Auditorium, Austin

12
Convention Center, San Antonio

14
Civic Center, Monroe, La.

17
Freedom Hall, Johnson City, Tenn.

18
Coliseum, Knoxville

20
University of Alabama Coliseum, Tuscaloosa

21
Omni, Atlanta

22
Municipal Auditorium, Mobile

24
William and Mary University, Williamsburg, Va.

25
Mosque, Richmond

26
Capitol Center, Washington

28
Civic Center, Providence

29
Veterans Memorial Coliseum, New Haven

30
Spectrum, Philadelphia. Eric flies home for a break.

MAY 1979
20
Eric and Pattie celebrate their

wedding with a huge party at their home. Paul McCartney, Ringo Starr, George Harrison, Denny Laine, and Jack Bruce are among the two hundred guests and all play with Eric in a marquee in the grounds of his home.

25
Civic Center, Augusta, Maine

26
Cumberland County Civic Center, Portland, Maine

28
Civic Center, Binghamton, N.Y.

29
War Memorial Arena, Syracuse

30
War Memorial, Rochester

JUNE 1979
1
Memorial Auditorium, Buffalo

2
Richfield Coliseum, Cleveland

4
Sports Arena, Toledo

5
Civic Center, Saginaw, Mich.

7
Riverfront Coliseum, Cincinnati

8
Market Square Arena, Indianapolis

9
Dane County Exposition Center, Madison, Wisc.

10
Civic Center, St. Paul

12
Chicago Stadium, Chicago. Eric jams with Muddy Waters on "Got My Mojo Working." Muddy Waters and Johnny Winter jam with Eric on "Long Distance Call" and "Kansas City."

13
Wings Stadium, Kalamazoo

15
Notre Dame University, South Bend

Top: With Muddy Waters, Dingwalls, London, December 1978. (Paul Slattery)

Center: At Glyn Johns's wedding, 1978. (LFI)

16
Brown County Veterans Memorial Coliseum, Green Bay, Wisc.

18
Civic Auditorium, Omaha

19
Kansas Coliseum, Wichita

21
Salt Palace, Salt Lake City

23
Coliseum, Spokane

24
Coliseum, Seattle. Marc Benno releases his *Lost in Austin* LP. Eric plays on "Hotfoot Blues," "Chasin' Rainbows," "Me and a Friend of Mine," "New Romance," "Last Train," "Lost in Austin," "Splish Splash," "Monterey Pen," "The Drifter," "Hey There Señorita."

AUGUST 1979
Danny Douma releases his *Night Eyes* album. Eric plays on "Hate You."

SEPTEMBER 1979
Eric premieres his all new British band which now consists of Albert Lee (guitar and vocals), Henri Spinetti (drums), Dave Markee (bass), and Chris Stainton (keyboards). They embark on a world tour.

30
Victoria Hall, Hanley. The sets include the following songs: "Badge," "Worried Life Blues," "If I Don't Be There by Morning," "Tulsa Time," "Early in the Morning," "Watch Out for Lucy," "Wonderful Tonight," "Setting Me Up," "La La La," "Lay Down Sally," "All Our Past Times," "Double Trouble," "After Midnight," "Key to the Highway," "Knockin' on Heaven's Door," "Country Boy," "Cocaine," "Further on Up the Road," and "Blues Power."

OCTOBER 1979
6
Stadthalle, Vienna

7
Sporthalle, Linz

8
Messehalle, Nuremberg. The tour continues in Yugoslavia and Poland: The Palata Pioneer Hall in Belgrade, two shows at the Dom Sportover in Zagreb, the Palace of Culture in Warsaw, and the Katowice Stadium, which was a disastrous concert for Eric due to police brutality toward fans.

10
Palata Pioneer Hall, Belgrade

11, 12
Dom Sportover, Zagreb

15, 16
Salo Kongresso, Warsaw

17, 18
Halo Sportowo, Katowice, Poland (second concert cancelled due to police induced riot)

Eric Clapton: **How can I play when I see kids right in front of the stage, underneath me, being pushed about by the men from Sainsbury's. [That's what Eric called the police guards.] Anywhere else in the world we could help the kids by telling them to cool it. But there, I'm powerless because of the language problem and because the authorities are so heavy. The whole place reminds me of the Third Man.**

The tour continues to Israel with five shows.

21, 22, 23, 25
Heichal Hatarbut, Tel Aviv

27
Binyanei Ha'Ooma, Jerusalem

NOVEMBER 1979
After a well deserved break, Eric and his band continued their world tour. The set for this part would normally run as follows: "Tulsa Time," "Early in the Morning," "Lay Down Sally," "Wonderful Tonight," "If I Don't Be There by Morning," "Worried Life Blues," "Country Boy," "All Our Pastimes," "Blues Power," "Knockin' on Heaven's Door," "Settin' Me Up," "Ramblin' on My Mind," "After Midnight," "Cocaine," "Layla," and "Further on Up the Road."

The tour resumes and continues in the Far East.

16
National Theatre, Bangkok

18
Araneta Coliseum Cinema, Manila

20
Academic Hall, Hong Kong

1979/ 1980

23
Kemin Bunka Center, Ibaragi, Japan

25
Shikokaido, Nagoya

26
Kaikan Hall, Kyoto

27
Koseinenkin Hall, Osaka

28
Yubin Chokin Hall, Hiroshima

30
Shin-Nittetsu Taiiku-Kan, Kokura

DECEMBER 1979

1
Furitsu Taiiku-Kan, Osaka

2, 3
Budokan, Tokyo. (Live recording of *Just One Night* double album.)

6
Kyoshin Kaijo, Sapporo

FEBRUARY 1980

Gary Brooker releases "Home Lovin'," backed with "Chasing The Chop." Eric plays on both.

MARCH 1980

Alexis Korner releases his *Party Album.* Eric plays on "Hey Pretty Mama," "Hi-Heel Sneakers," and "They Call It Stormy Monday." This double album is released only in Germany.

APRIL 1980

Gary Brooker joins Eric's band. Recording begins at Surrey Sound Studios.

Gary Brooker releases "Leave the Candle" as a single. Eric plays on the A-side.

MAY 1980

British tour opens in Oxford. The set normally runs as follows: "Tulsa Time," "Early in the Morning," "Lay Down Sally," "Wonderful Tonight," "Country Boy," "Thunder and Lightning," "Blues Power," "All Our Pastimes," "Setting Me Up," "Leave the Candle," "If I Don't Be There by Morning," "Ramblin' on My Mind," "Have You Ever Loved a Woman," "After Midnight," "Cocaine," "Layla," and "Further on Up the Road."

2
New Theatre, Oxford

3
Brighton Centre, Brighton

4
Bingley Hall, Stafford

7
City Hall, Newcastle-upon-Tyne

8
Odeon, Edinburgh

9
Apollo, Glasgow

11
Leisure Centre, Deeside

12
Coventry Theatre, Coventry

13
Hippodrome, Bristol

15, 16, 17
Hammersmith Odeon, London

18
Civic Hall, Guildford. Jeff Beck jams with Eric on

"Ramblin' on My Mind." Eric and Albert Lee jam with Chas and Dave on "Roll Over Beethoven." Chas and Dave support Eric on the tour.

Eric releases his live double LP *Just One Night* recorded at the Budokan, Tokyo, December 1979.

JULY 1980

Ronnie Lane releases his *See Me* album. Eric plays on "Lad's Got Money," "Barcelona," and "Way Up Yonder."

Eric and band head off to Compass Point Studios in Nassau to begin recording a new studio LP.

SEPTEMBER 1980

Scandinavian tour. Band is same as British tour.

19
Aalborghall, Allborg

20
Broendbyhall, Copenhagen

21
Vejlbyrisskovhall, Aarhus

23
Olympen, Lund

24
Scandinavium, Gothenberg

25
Drammenshall, Oslo

27
Isstadion, Stockholm

Right: Posing for sleeve shot of Just One Night.

JUST ONE NIGHT

UK RSDX 2
US RSO RS 2-4202
Released May 1980

Side One:
1. Tulsa Time
2. Early in the Morning
3. Lay Down Sally
4. Wonderful Tonight

Side Two:
5. If I Don't Be There by Morning
6. Worried Life Blues
7. All Our Pasttimes
8. After Midnight

Side Three:
9. Double Trouble
10. Setting Me Up
11. Blues Power

Side Four:
12. Ramblin' on My Mind
13. Cocaine
14. Further on Up the Road

ERIC CLAPTON
JUST ONE NIGHT

RAINBOW

GUILDFORD CIVIC HALL
HARVEY GOLDSMITH PRESENTS
ERIC CLAPTO
AND HIS BA
THIS SPECIAL GUESTS
CHAS and DR
Sunday 18th May 1:00
ALL TICKETS £3.00
№ 0369

1981

Top and center: At *The Secret Policeman's Other Ball,* Drury Lane Theatre, London, September 1981. (Michael Putland)

ANOTHER TICKET

UK RSO 5008
US RSO RX 1-3095
Released February 1981

Side One:
1. Something Special
2. Black Rose
3. Blow Wind Blow
4. Another Ticket
5. I Can't Stand It
Side Two:
6. Hold Me Lord
7. Floating Bridge
8. Catch Me If You Can
9. Rita Mae

29
Icehall, Helsinki

JANUARY 1981

Start of short Irish tour followed by a one-off London show. "Whiter Shade of Pale" added to the set.

31
Simmonscourt, Dublin

FEBRUARY 1981

1
Leisureland, Galway

2
City Hall, Cork

3
Youree Youth Centre, Carlow

5
The Rainbow, London. Eric releases "I Can't Stand It" backed with "Black Rose" as a single. He also releases a new album *Another Ticket.*

Phil Collins releases his *Face Value* LP. Eric plays on "If Leaving Me Is Easy."

MARCH 1981

Start of huge U.S. tour which is cut short due to illness. "Rita Mae" added to the set.

2
Memorial Coliseum, Portland, Ore.

3
The Coliseum, Spokane

5, 6, 7
Paramount Theater, Seattle.

9
Yellowstone Metra, Billings, Mont.

10
The Four Seasons Arena, Great Falls, Mont.

13
Dane County Exposition Center, Madison, Wisc.

14
Eric is rushed to the hospital for treatment for ulcers, one of which is later described by

doctors as "as big as an orange." Forty-seven concerts are cancelled. Eric was seriously ill, very close to dying, and would not reappear in public until September.

APRIL 1981

Eric releases "Another Ticket" backed with "Rita Mae" as a single.

SEPTEMBER 1981

Charity concerts for Amnesty International:

9
Theatre Royal, Drury Lane, London. Eric plays with Jeff Beck on "Cause We Ended as Lovers" and "Crossroads."

They join the rest of the artists for "I Shall Be Released."

10
Theatre Royal, Drury Lane, London. Eric plays with Jeff Beck on "Cause We Ended As Lovers" and "Further on Up the Road." They join the rest

of the artists for "I Shall Be Released."

12

Theatre Royal, Drury Lane, London. Eric and Jeff Beck join the other artists for "I Shall Be Released."

Other musicians appearing at these shows include Midge Ure, Sting, Donovan, and Phil Collins. Comedians include Billy Connolly, John Cleese, Rowan Atkinson, Pamela Stephenson, and Alexi Sayle.

John Martyn releases his *Glorious Fool* LP. Eric plays on "Couldn't Love You More."

Stack-O-Hits Records releases *All Night Boogie* by Howlin' Wolf. This gem consists of outtakes from *The London Sessions*. Eric plays on all tracks.

OCTOBER 1981

The set for the upcoming Scandinavian tour runs as

follows: "Tulsa Time," "Lay Down Sally," "Wonderful Tonight," "Worried Life Blues," "After Midnight," "Whiter Shade of Pale," "Country Boy," "Double Trouble," "Rita Mae," "Knockin' on Heaven's Door," "Blues Power," "Ramblin' on My Mind," "Have You Ever Loved a Woman," "Cocaine," "Layla," and "Further on Up the Road."

7

Icehall, Helsinki

9

Isstadion, Stockholm

10

Scandinavium, Gothenburg

12

Drammenshall, Oslo

13

Olympen, Lund

15

Forum, Copenhagen

16

Vejlbyrissnovhall, Aarhus

17

Randers Hallen, Randers. Eric plays saxophone on "Further on Up the Road" and renames "Cocaine" "Cornflakes."

NOVEMBER 1981

16

Civic Hall, Wolverhampton. Eric plays one-off gig for the John Wile (West Bromwich Albion soccer player) testimonial before heading off to tour Japan.

19, 20

Shepperton Studios. Rehearsals for Japanese tour.

The set for the Japanese tour normally ran as follows: "Tulsa Time," "Lay Down Sally," "Wonderful Tonight,"

Top far left: Rehearsals for *The Secret Policeman's Other Ball* with Jeff Beck and Sting. (Michael Putland)

Bottom left: *SPOB* with Jeff Beck and Neil Murray. (Michael Putland)

Bottom right: Backstage at Drury Lane, September 1981, with Sting, and Jeff Beck. (Adrian Boot)

1981/ 1982

"After Midnight," "I Shot the Sheriff," "Whiter Shade of Pale," "Setting Me Up," "Another Ticket," "Blues Power," "Badge," "Motherless Children," "Ramblin' on My Mind," "Have You Ever Loved a Woman," "Cocaine," "Layla," and "Further on Up the Road."

27

Kenmin Hall, Niigata

30

Dichi Koseinenkin Hall, Nagoya

DECEMBER 1981

1

Festival Hall, Osaka

3

Sun Palace, Fukuoka

4

Kaikan Dai-Ichi Hall, Kyoto

7

Budokan, Tokyo

8

Bunka Taiiku-Kan, Yokohama

9

Budokan, Tokyo

MARCH 1982

A very quiet year for Eric which is spent curing his drinking problem and restoring his health.

Eric Clapton: It was pointed out to me while I was in hospital that I had a drink problem, and I think that was the first time anyone had ever said something like that to me. But I was still happy drinking and quite terrified of not drinking. I had to go further down that road to complete insanity before I stopped.

Gary Brooker releases his *Lead Me to the Water* LP. Eric plays on the title track.

The Secret Policeman's Other Ball—The Music LP released. Eric plays on "Cause We Ended as Lovers," "Further on Up the Road," "Crossroads," and "I Shall Be Released."

MAY 1982

18

Eric is interviewed on BBC1 after his horse *The Ripleyite* wins the three o'clock at Goodwood races.

Eric attends a Ry Cooder show at Hammersmith Odeon in London.

JUNE 1982

Eric undertakes his only tour of the year. The band is unchanged and the set runs as follows: "Tulsa Time," "Lay Down Sally," "I Shot the Sheriff," "Blow Wind Blow," "Wonderful Tonight," "Pink Bedroom," "Whiter Shade of Pale," "Key to the Highway," "Double Trouble," "Blues Power," "Cocaine," "Layla," and "Further on Up the Road."

5

Paramount Theater, Cedar Rapids, Iowa

6

Civic Auditorium, Omaha

7

Metropolitan Center, Minneapolis

10, 11

Pine Knob Pavilion, Detroit

12

Memorial Auditorium, Buffalo

13

Blossom Music Center,
Cleveland

17

Cumberland County Civic
Center, Portland, Me.

18

Broome County Coliseum,
Binghamton, N.Y.

19

Performing Arts Center,
Saratoga, N.Y.

22

Hampton Roads Coliseum,
Hampton Roads, Va.

23

Coliseum, Charlotte, N.C.

24

Viking Hall, Bristol, Tenn.

27

Civic Center, Augusta, Ga.

28

Coliseum, Jacksonville, Fla.

29

Civic Center, Lakeland, Fla.

30

Sportatorium, Miami. Muddy
Waters jams with Eric on
"Blow Wind Blow." Sadly, this
turned out to be Muddy's last
live appearance.

SEPTEMBER– NOVEMBER 1982

Eric replaces his English
rhythm section with American
musicians.

Eric records his new LP at
Compass Point Studios,
Nassau, with Duck Dunn
(bass), Roger Hawkins
(drums), Albert Lee (guitar,
keyboards), and Ry Cooder
(guitar).

DECEMBER 1982

22

Eric plays The Royal Pub in
Guildford, Surrey.

1983

JANUARY 1983

Eric rehearses with his new band for a huge tour. Chris Stainton rejoins the group.

"I've Got A Rock 'n' Roll Heart" backed with "Man in Love" released as Eric's new single.

FEBRUARY 1983

Eric's band now features Duck Dunn (bass), Roger Hawkins (drums), Albert Lee (guitar, keyboards), and Chris Stainton (keyboards). Ry Cooder is support act for the U.S. tour.

The set for the first half of the tour is as follows: "After Midnight," "I Shot the Sheriff," "Worried Life Blues," "Crazy Country Hop," "Crosscut Saw," "Slow Down Linda," "Sweet Little Lisa," "Key to the Highway," "Tulsa Time," "Rock 'n' Roll Heart," "Wonderful Tonight," "Blues Power," "Who's Lovin' You Tonight," "Have You Ever Loved a Woman," "Ramblin' on My Mind," "Let It Rain," "Cocaine," "Layla," and "Further on Up the Road."

The tour is promoted by Camel cigarettes, which causes various health-related organizations to complain.

Nat Walker **(Camel Cigarettes): We felt that the music of a guy like Eric Clapton fits the interest profile of a Camel smoker. Music is important to the Camel brand.**

1, 2

Paramount Theater, Seattle. Eric plays "Pretty Girl" and "Nobody Knows You When You're Down and Out" during his set.

3

Cumberland County Civic Center, Portland, Ore.

6

Convention Center, Sacramento

7

Cow Palace, San Francisco

8

Universal Amphitheater, Los Angeles

9

Arena, Long Beach

11

Veterans Memorial Coliseum, Phoenix

13

Erwin Events Center, Austin

14

The Summit, Houston

15

Reunion Arena, Dallas. Last show with Roger Hawkins. He is replaced by Jamie Oldaker.

17

Mid-South Coliseum, Memphis

18

Kiel Auditorium, St. Louis

19

Hara Arena, Dayton

21

Spectrum, Philadelphia. Ry Cooder jams with Eric on "Crossroads."

22

Meadowlands Arena, East Rutherford, N.J.

25

Omni, Atlanta

26

The Gardens, Louisville

28

Capital Center, Washington. Eric's new album *Money and Cigarettes* is released.

MARCH 1983

1

Centrum, Worcester, Mass.

2

Hershey Park Arena, Hershey, Pa.

MONEY AND CIGARETTES

UK W 3773
US Warner Bros/Duck Records 123773
Released February 1983

Side One:
1. Everybody Oughta Make a Change
2. The Shape You're In
3. Aren't Going Down
4. I've Got a Rock'n'Roll Heart
5. Man Overboard

Side Two:
6. Pretty Girl
7. Man in Love
8. Crosscut Saw
9. Slow Down Linda
10. Crazy Country Hop

ERIC CLAPTON AND HIS BAND

Friday April 8th and
Saturday April 9th Edinburgh Playhouse
£6.50 £5.50 Box Office 031-557 2590

Monday April 11th Newcastle City Hall
£6.50 £5.50 Box Office 0632 320007

Tuesday April 12th Liverpool Empire
£6.50 £5.50 Box Office 051-708 7714

Friday May 13th
St. Austell Cornwall Coliseum
£6.50 £5.50 Box Office 072681 4261

Saturday May 14th Poole Arts Centre
£5.50 Box Office 0202 670521

Above: Hammersmith Odeon, May 1983. (Barry Plummer)

3

Civic Arena, Pittsburgh. "The Shape You're In" backed with "Crosscut Saw" released as Eric's new single.

APRIL 1983

Start of British and European tour before continuing in the U.S. The set is as follows: "Tulsa Time," "I Shot the Sheriff," "Worried Life Blues," "Lay Down Sally," "Let It Rain," "Double Trouble," "Sweet Little Lisa," "Key to the Highway," "After Midnight," "The Shape You're In," "Wonderful Tonight," "Blues Power," "Ramblin' on My Mind," "Have You Ever Loved a Woman," "Cocaine," "Layla," and "Further on Up the Road."

8, 9

Playhouse, Edinburgh

11

City Hall, Newcastle-upon-Tyne

12

Empire, Liverpool

14, 15, 16

National Stadium, Dublin

20

Stadthalle, Bremen

21

Grugahalle, Essen

23

Ahoy Hall, Rotterdam

24

Chapitau De Pantin, Paris

26

Sportshalle, Cologne

27

Festhalle, Frankfurt

29

Rhein-Neckar-Halle, Eppelheim

30

St. Jakobshalle, Basle

MAY 1983

2

Palaeur, Rome

3

Palazzo Dello Sport, Genoa

5

Palais Des Sport, Toulouse

7

Palacio Municipal De Deportes, Barcelona

8

Velodromo Anoeta, San Sebastian

13

Coliseum, St. Austell

89

1983

14

Arts Centre, Poole

16, 17, 18, 19

Hammersmith Odeon, London

21

Apollo, Manchester

22

De Montfort Hall, Leicester

23

Civic Hall, Guildford. This is another of the very special hometown shows that Eric occasionally plays for his family, friends, and locals.

The set is "Tulsa Time," "I Shot the Sheriff," "Worried Life Blues," "Lay Down Sally," "Let It Rain," "Double Trouble," "Sweet Little Lisa," "The Shape You're In," "Wonderful Tonight," "Blues Power," "Sad Sad Day," "Have You Ever Loved a Woman," "Ramblin' on My Mind," and "Layla."

Encores of "Further on Up the Road" and "Cocaine" feature Phil Collins (drums) and Jimmy Page (guitar). "Roll Over Beethoven" follows with Chas and Dave, followed by "You Won Again," "Matchbox," and "Goodnight Irene" with Paul Brady joining the rest of this special ad hoc band.

"Slow Down Linda" backed with "Crazy Country Hop" is released as Eric's new single.

JUNE 1983

5

New Victoria Theatre, London. Eric joins Chas and Dave, Richard Digance, and Jim Davidson for a "Save the Children" benefit.

24

Eric is presented with the year's Silver Clef award for Outstanding Achievement in the World of British Music by Princess Michael of Kent at the eighth Music Therapy Charity lunch in London.

25

Kingswood Music Theater, Toronto

27, 28, 29

Pine Knob Pavilion, Detroit. Ringo Starr releases his *Old Wave* album. Eric plays on "Everybody's in a Hurry But Me."

JULY 1983

1

Performing Arts Center, Saratoga, N.Y.

2, 3

Jones Beach, Wantaugh, N.Y.

5

Merriweather Post Pavilion, Columbia, S.C.

7

Blossom Music Center, Cleveland

9

Civic Center Arena, St. Paul

10

Summerfest, Milwaukee

11

Poplar Creek, Chicago. After this show, Eric goes to the Checker Board lounge where he jams with Buddy Guy.

13

Kings Island Timberwolf Theater, Cincinnati

14

Wings Stadium, Kalamazoo

16, 17

Red Rocks, Denver. On 17, The Blasters join Eric on "Further on Up the Road."

Eric Clapton: I am much more out front now, and I do feel much more confident. I know what I can do, yet I know my limits. When I'm playing well it knocks me out.

AUGUST 1983

The press announces that Eric will be doing two charity shows in September to

All shots from Hammersmith Odeon, May 1983. (Barry Plummer)

1983

celebrate twenty years in the business.

Eric helps out Roger Waters, formerly of Pink Floyd, for the recording of his *Pros and Cons of Hitch-Hiking* album.

SEPTEMBER 1983
20

Royal Albert Hall, London (Ronnie Lane/Arms Benefits). The set consists of "Everybody Oughta Make a Change," "Lay Down Sally," "Wonderful Tonight," "Ramblin' on My Mind," "Have You Ever Loved a Woman," "Rita Mae," "Cocaine," and "Man Smart Woman Smarter." Eric then accompanies Stevie Winwood on "Hound Dog," "Best That I Can," "Road Runner," "Slowdown Sundown," "Take Me to the River," and "Gimme Some Lovin'."

After an interval, Jeff Beck performs "Star Cycle,"

"Pump," "Led Boots," "Goodbye Pork Pie Hat," "People Get Ready," and "Hi Ho Silver Lining," and Jimmy Page performs "Prelude," "Who's to Blame," "City Sirens," and "Stairway to Heaven." Neither set features Eric. After Page's last number, Eric and Jeff return to the stage for the remainder of the show together with Page. They perform "Tulsa Time," "Wee Wee Baby," and "Layla." Ronnie Lane comes out for the final two numbers, "Bomber's Moon" and "Goodnight Irene."

A very emotional and historic night which is videoed for later release.

21

Royal Albert Hall, London (Prince's Trust). Eric's set for this show is: "Everybody Oughta Make a Change," "Lay Down Sally," "Ramblin'

on My Mind," "Have You Ever Loved a Woman," "Rita Mae," "Cocaine," and "Man Smart Woman Smarter." Eric's set is followed by Stevie Winwood performing "The Best That I Can," "Road Runner," "Slowdown Sundown," "Take Me to the River," and "Gimme Some Lovin'," all featuring Eric. Jeff Beck's and Jimmy Page's sets follow. The whole band returns for "Wee Wee Baby" and "Layla." Ronnie Lane comes out for the final number, "Goodnight Irene."

A much shorter set than the previous night, probably because Prince Charles and Princess Diana are in the Royal Box. It's still a great show though.

The backing band for these two shows comprises: Andy Fairweather Low (guitar, vocals), Kenney Jones (drums), Charlie Watts (drums), Bill Wyman (bass), Ray Cooper (percussion), Chris Stainton (keyboards), James Hooker (keyboards), Fernando Saunders (bass), and Simon Phillips (drums).

Eric Clapton: **Obviously it was a concert I very much wanted to do both on behalf of Ronnie [Lane], and on behalf of the Action Research into Multiple Sclerosis Fund. But that didn't mean I wasn't nervous. Far from it, I was petrified when we had the first rehearsals. But it rapidly became great fun. And it was a delight to**

Top: At the Royal Albert Hall ARMS concert, September 21, 1983. (LFI)

Center: ARMS concert, September 20, with Bill Wyman. (Andre Csillag)

Bottom: ARMS show, September 20, with Bill Wyman and Jeff Beck. (Andre Csillag)

work with such a competent bunch of musicians.

Originally, the idea was for everyone to just sort of loosely jam together, but subsequently it was quite rightly decided that everyone involved should do their own little regular sets, with the rest of the band providing the backing.

OCTOBER 1983

The press announces the Albert Hall supergroup will do a short tour of America for ARMS.

Bill Wyman: We all had such a great time at the Albert Hall we decided to carry on. We thought it would have been a shame to have simply gone our separate ways. The meeting was much easier to arrange than any I've had with the Stones. We were all there bang on eleven o'clock. With the Stones eleven o'clock on Wednesday usually means nine o'clock on Friday.

NOVEMBER 1983

Eric attends the opening of the Hippodrome among a host of stars. Stevie Winwood is

unable to do the U.S. ARMS dates and is replaced by Joe Cocker. Paul Rogers also joins the lineup as does Jan Hammer. The backing band remains the same as for the Albert Hall.

The set for the U.S. shows runs as follows: "Everybody Oughta Make a Change," "Lay Down Sally," "Wonderful Tonight," "Rita Mae," "Sad Sad Day," "Have You Ever Loved a Woman," "Ramblin' on My Mind," and "Cocaine." Eric's set is followed by Joe Cocker performing "Don't Talk to Me," "Watching the River Flow," "Worried Life

Blues," "You Are So Beautiful," "Seven Days," and "Feelin' Alright." Eric is featured on all. Jeff Beck follows as does Jimmy Page who performs "Stairway to Heaven" at the end of his set. Unlike in England, he is joined by Jeff Beck and Eric for some great guitar dueling during Led Zeppelin's anthem. The whole band returns to perform "Layla" and "With a Little Help From My Friends." Ronnie Lane comes out to perform "April Fool" and "Goodnight Irene" accompanied by the whole cast.

1983/ 1984

28, 29

Reunion Arena, Dallas. After the show, Eric goes to the Tango Club with Bill Wyman to jam with Lonnie Mack.

DECEMBER 1983
1, 2, 3

Cow Palace, San Francisco

5, 6

The Forum, Los Angeles. After the show, Eric, Jeff Beck, and Ron Wood go to the Baked Potato Club to watch Duane Eddy.

8, 9

Madison Square Garden, New York. Ronnie Wood joins Eric on "Cocaine" and the encores.

Bill Graham: Neal Schon [of Journey] was here last night, and he said, "Bill—we should do this. The young musicians.

We could get Carlos Santana and Eddie Van Halen and myself together . . ." And I said, "Come onnnnn, are you kidding? Which part would you play?"

JANUARY 1984
15, 16, 17, 18

Eric rehearses for an upcoming tour.

The set for this tour is as follows: "Everybody Oughta Make a Change," "Motherless Children," "I Shot the Sheriff," "The Sky Is Crying," "Badge," "The Shape You're In," "Same Old Blues," "Rita Mae," "Blow Wind Blow," "Wonderful Tonight," "Let It Rain," "Key to the Highway," "Sweet Little Lisa," "Double Trouble," "Tulsa Time," "Bottle of Red Wine," "Honey Bee," "Have You Ever Loved a Woman," "Ramblin' On My

All shots from Roger Waters's tour, June 1984. (Barry Plummer)

Mind," "Cocaine," "Layla," and "Further on Up the Road."

The band is the same as the 1983 tour.

20, 21
Hallenstadion, Zurich

23, 24
Teatrotenda, Milan

26
Beogradski-Sajam Hala, Belgrade

28, 29
Sporting of Athens, Athens

FEBRUARY 1984
2
American University, Cairo

5, 6
Binyanei Ha'Ooma, Jerusalem

7
Returns to England.

MARCH 1984
Eric flies to Montserrat with (producer) Phil Collins for the recording of his next LP.

Tracks that Eric records are: "Too Bad," "She's Waiting," "Same Old Blues," "Knock on Wood," "It All Depends," "Tangled in Love," "Never Make You Cry," "Just Like a Prisoner," "Jailbreak," "Heaven's Just One Step Away," "You Don't Know Like I Know" (a duet with Phil Collins).

APRIL 1984
More recording at Montserrat Air Studios. Roger Waters releases his *Pros and Cons of Hitch-Hiking* LP. Eric plays on all tracks.

MAY 1984
Rehearsals for the forthcoming Roger Waters tour.

JUNE 1984
The band for the Roger Waters tour comprises Waters (bass, vocals), Tim Renwick

1984

(guitar), Michael Kamen (keyboards), Andy Newmark (drums), Mel Collins (sax), Doreen Chanter (backing vocals), Katie Kissoon (backing vocals), Chris Stainton (keyboards), and Eric Clapton (guitar, vocals).

The set for the tour is as follows: Part 1—"Set the Controls for the Heart of the Sun," "Money," "If," "Welcome to the Machine," "Have a Cigar," "Wish You Were Here," "Pigs on the Wing," "In the Flesh," "Nobody Home," "Hey You," and "The Gunner's Dream." Part 2— "4:30 a.m. (Apparently They Were Travelling Abroad)," "4:33 a.m. (Running Shoes)," "4:37 a.m. (Arabs With Knives and West German Skies)," "4:39 a.m. (For the First Time Today—Part 2)," "4:41 a.m. (Sexual Revolution)," "4:47 a.m. (The Remains of Our Love)," "4:50 a.m. (Go Fishing)," "4:56 a.m. (For the First Time Today— Part 1)," "4:58 a.m. (Dunroamin, Duncarin, Dunlivin)," "5:01 a.m. (The Pros and Cons of Hitch-Hiking)," "5:06 a.m. (Every Stranger's Eyes)," "5:11 a.m. (The Moment of Clarity)." The encore is "Brain Damage."

Eric undertakes this tour against the wishes of his management, but to an outsider it provides the listener with some of his finest playing because he is not under the pressure of being permanently in the spotlight.

16, 17
Isstadion, Stockholm

19
Ahoy Theatre, Rotterdam

21, 22
Earls Court, London

26, 27
NEC, Birmingham. Corey Hart releases his solo LP. Eric plays on "Jenny Fey."

JULY 1984
3
Hallenstadium, Zurich

6
Palais Des Sport, Paris. End of tour. U.S. tour to follow.

7

Wembley Stadium, London. Eric jams with Bob Dylan alongside Carlos Santana, Chrissie Hynde, Van Morrison, and Mick Taylor on "Leopard Skin Pillbox Hat," "It's All Over Now Baby Blue," "Tombstone Blues," "Señor," "The Times They Are A-Changin'," "Blowin' in the Wind," and "Knockin' on Heaven's Door."

Eric attends the launch of "The Ronnie Lane Appeal For Arms Concert" video at a London hotel together with Bill Wyman, Andy Fairweather Low, Kenny Jones, Stevie Winwood, and Ronnie Lane.

17, 18

Civic Center, Hartford.
U.S. leg of the Roger Waters tour.

20, 21, 22

Meadowlands Arena, East Rutherford, N.J.

24

The Spectrum, Philadelphia

26

Stadium, Chicago

28, 29

Maple Leaf Gardens, Toronto

31

The Forum, Montreal. Although Roger Waters plays further American dates the

following year, Eric has by this time left his band.

AUGUST 1984
4

Phil Collins marries. The marquee in the back of his garden finds Collins jamming with Eric, Robert Plant, and Peter Gabriel.

OCTOBER 1984

Eric spends most of the month rehearsing for his upcoming Australasian tour. Albert Lee is no longer in the band.

NOVEMBER 1984

Eric's band now comprises: Eric (guitar, vocals), Chris Stainton (keyboards), Jamie Oldaker (drums), Duck Dunn (bass), Marcy Levy (backing vocals), Shaun Murphy (backing vocals), and Peter Robinson (synthesizer).

The set for the tour is as follows: "Everybody Oughta Make a Change," "Motherless Children," "I Shot the Sheriff," "Same Old Blues," "Tangled in Love," "She's

Waiting," "Steppin' Out," "Tulsa Time," "Badge," "Love Sign," "Wonderful Tonight," "Let It Rain," "Who's Loving You Tonight," "Have You Ever Loved a Woman," "Ramblin' on My Mind," "Cocaine," "Layla," "Knock on Wood," and "You Don't Know Like I Know."

13, 14

Hordern Pavilion, Sydney

17

Festival Hall, Brisbane

20, 21

Hordern Pavilion, Sydney

23, 24, 25

Sports and Entertainment Centre, Melbourne

28

Entertainments Centre, Perth. "You Don't Know Like I Know," a duet with Eric and Phil Collins, released in Australia to coincide with the tour. It has not been released elsewhere.

1984/ 1985

An amusing incident happens in Perth. Angry at being awakened at some ungodly hour by Ritchie Blackmore's impromptu jam session in the Sheraton Hotel, Eric sends his minder Alfie to sort things out. Shouldering his way into Ritchie's room, he warns "If I have to come back here there's going to be a stoush." Needless to say, silence reigned supreme. Alfie's stature is rather on the large side.

DECEMBER 1984

Eric records some further tracks for his new album at Lion Share Studios in Los Angeles. Tracks recorded are "Forever Man," "See What Love Can Do," "Something's Happening," and "Loving Your Lovin'." These more commercial tracks were done at Warners' request as they felt the previous material did not offer enough singles material to release. Eric also records "Behind The Sun" at home as a last minute inclusion with which to finish the album.

2

The Coliseum, Hong Kong. End of tour.

Eric attends one of Nik

Top right and below: Wembley Arena, March 4, 1985. (Stuart Pearsall).

Bottom: With Pattie at the premiere of *Brazil*. (LFI)

Kershaw's concerts at Hammersmith Odeon.

JANUARY 1985
2

Eric attends Ronnie Wood's wedding in Denham. Eric films his first ever video for an upcoming single "Forever Man."

FEBRUARY 1985
17

Attends premiere of Terry Gilliam's film *Brazil*.

18

Eric rehearses for his upcoming world tour. Tim Renwick is added to the band on guitar and Peter Robinson leaves.

The set for the British and Scandinavian tour is as follows: "Everybody Oughta Make a Change," "Motherless Children," "I Shot the Sheriff," "Same Old Blues," "Blues Power," "Tangled in Love," "Steppin' Out," "Just Like a Prisoner," "Tulsa Time," "Something Is Wrong With My Baby," "Badge," "Behind the Sun," "Wonderful Tonight," "Let It Rain," "Who's Lovin' You Tonight," "Have You Ever Loved a Woman," "Ramblin' on My Mind," "Cocaine," "Layla," "Knock on Wood," and "Further on Up the Road."

This whole tour sees Eric playing at his volatile best; in fact he's never played better.

27, 28

The Playhouse, Edinburgh. "Forever Man" backed with "Too Bad" released as Eric's new single. 12-inch has extra track, "Heaven Is One Step Away."

MARCH 1985

Eric flies to Montserrat with Phil Collins for the recording of his next album. Sessions take place at Air Studios with Phil producing as well as providing drumming on some numbers.

Tracks recorded are: "You Don't Know Like I Know," "Knock on Wood," "Heaven Is One Step Away," "Too Bad," "One Jump Ahead of the Storm," "Same Old Blues," "She's Waiting," "It All Depends," "Tangled in Love," "Never Make You Cry," "Just Like a Prisoner," "Jailbait."

He also records a few numbers with Stephen Bishop at the same sessions. One of these is "Hall Light."

1, 2

NEC, Birmingham. "Lay Down Sally" replaces "Just Like a Prisoner" from March 2 onward.

4, 5

Wembley Arena, London. On 5 Dan Aykroyd jams with Eric on "Further on Up the Road."

ERIC CLAPTON AND HIS BAND

plus support

EDINBURGH PLAYHOUSE
WEDNESDAY 27th FEBRUARY
TICKETS £7.50 & £6.50 from Box Office and usual agents

BIRMINGHAM N.E.C.
SATURDAY 2nd MARCH
TICKETS £7.50 & £6.50

WEMBLEY ARENA
MONDAY 4th MARCH

Left: USA, April 1985.
(Retna)

1985

Right: Wembley Arena, March 4, 1985. (David Redfern)

BEHIND THE SUN

UK Duck Records 925 166-1
US Warner Bros/Duck Records 125661
Released March 1985

Side One:
1. She's Waiting
2. See What Love Can Do
3. Same Old Blues
4. Knock on Wood
5. Something's Happening

Side Two:
6. Forever Man
7. It All Depends
8. Tangled in Love
9. Never Make You Cry
10. Just Like a Prisoner
11. Behind the Sun

"You Don't Know Like I Know" added after "Knock on Wood."

9
Icehall, Helsinki

11
Scandinavium, Gothenburg

12
Valbyhallen, Copenhagen

14
Drammenshallen, Oslo

15
Isstadion, Stockholm. Eric's new LP *Behind the Sun* released; a fine album containing some of Eric's best guitar solos on record, particularly "Just Like a Prisoner."

Phil Collins: I think this album will surprise a lot of people. Eric took a Prophet and a Linn away to write the demos which is very unusual for him. He's also singing and playing better than I've ever heard him.

APRIL 1985

Start of American tour. The set for the first part of the American tour is as follows: "Tulsa Time," "Motherless Children," "I Shot the Sheriff," "Same Old Blues," "Blues Power," "Tangled in Love," "Behind the Sun," "Wonderful Tonight," "Steppin' Out," "Never Make You Cry," "She's Waiting," "Something Wrong With My Baby," "Lay Down Sally," "Badge," "Let It Rain," "Double Trouble," "Cocaine," "Layla," "Forever Man," and "Further on Up the Road."

9
Reunion Arena, Dallas

10
The Summit, Houston

11
Erwin Events Center, Austin

13
Civic Center, Pensacola

15
Civic Center, Lakeland. George Terry jams with his old boss.

16
James L. Knight Center, Miami

18
Duke University, Durham

19

Civic Center, Savannah

20

Omni, Atlanta. "Forever Man" played live for the first time.

22

Coliseum, Richmond, Va. This show is recorded for later radio broadcast.

23

Civic Center, Baltimore

25

Meadowlands Arena, East Rutherford, N.J.

26

Nassau Coliseum, Uniondale, N.Y.

28

Civic Center, Providence. Dick Sims jams with his old boss.

29

The Spectrum, Philadelphia

MAY 1985

1

Civic Center, Hartford. The show is filmed for video release.

2

Civic Center, Portland, Maine

3

The Forum, Montreal

8

Appears on *Late Night With David Letterman* and performs "Layla," "Lay Down Sally," "White Room," "Same Old Blues," "Forever Man," and "Knock on Wood" with the house band.

His performance of "White Room," the first time since Cream, inspires Eric to include it in his set for the second part of his tour.

The soundtrack to *Water* is released. Eric wrote the song "Freedom" and appears in the film along with George Harrison and Ringo Starr.

The set for the second part of the U.S. tour is as follows: "Tulsa Time," "Motherless Children," "I Shot the Sheriff," "Same Old Blues," "Tangled in Love," "White Room," "Steppin' Out," "Wonderful Tonight," "She's Waiting," "She Loves You," "Badge," "Let It Rain," "Double Trouble," "Cocaine," "Layla," "Forever Man," and "Further on Up the Road."

Eric returns to England to record his first soundtrack for the BBC drama *Edge of Darkness*.

JUNE 1985

21

Kingswood Music Theater, Toronto

22

Blossom Music Theater, Cleveland

23

Finger Lakes Music Center, Canandaigua, N.Y.

25

Performing Arts Center, Saratoga, N.Y.

26

The Centrum, Worcester, Mass.

27

Merriweather Post Pavilion, Columbia, Md.

28

Garden State Arts Center, Holmdel, N.J.

Top left: Backstage at the Live Aid concert, Philadelphia, July 13, 1985. (Retna)

Bottom: (LFI)

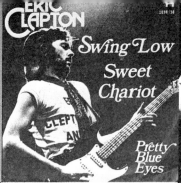

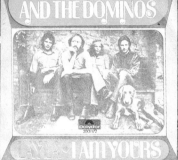

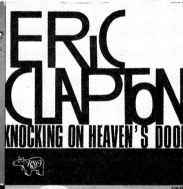

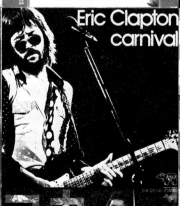

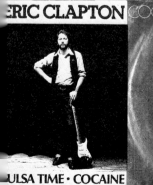

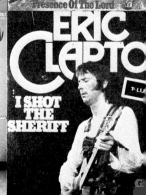

30

Summerfest, Milwaukee. "She's Waiting" backed with "Jailbait" released as Eric's new single.

JULY 1985

1

The Gardens, Louisville

2, 3

Pine Knob Pavilion, Detroit

5

Poplar Creek Music Theater, Chicago. After this show Eric jams with Buddy Guy for three sets at the Checker Board Lounge. (Anyone got tapes? That must have been something to see and hear . . .).

6

Music Amphitheater, Indianapolis

7

Riverbend Music Theater, Cincinnati

9

Sandstone Amphitheater, Kansas City, Kan.

11

Red Rocks Amphitheater, Denver

13

JFK Stadium, Philadelphia. This is the historic Live Aid Show. Eric plays "White Room," "She's Waiting," and "Layla" to millions. Eric also joins in the finale of "We Are the World" and adds some nice guitar lines.

14

Red Rocks Amphitheater, Denver

17, 18, 19

Universal Amphitheater, Los Angeles. Sergio Pastora Rodriguez jams with his old boss on the last night.

21

Compton Terrace, Phoenix

22

Pacific Amphitheater, Costa Mesa, Cal.

23, 24

Concord Pavilion, Concord, Cal. Carlos Santana jams with Eric on the first night.

26

Center Coliseum, Seattle. Lionel Richie joins Eric on stage for "Knock on Wood" and "You Don't Know Like I Know." Eric also recorded a guitar solo for Lionel's upcoming album.

27

PNE Coliseum, Vancouver. Lionel Richie jams with Eric on "Knock on Wood."

Singer Marcy Levy is replaced by Laura Creamer

for the remainder of the world tour.

AUGUST 1985

Month off.

SEPTEMBER 1985

Gary Brooker releases his *Echoes in the Night* LP. Eric plays on the title track.

OCTOBER 1985

1

Starts tour of Japan.

5, 6

Olympic Pool, Tokyo

7

Koseinenkin Hall, Osaka

9

Shimin Kaikan, Nagoya

10

Festival Hall, Osaka

11

Sun Palace, Fukuoka

14

George Sullivan Arena, Anchorage

20

Civic Hall, Guildford, Surrey. Phil Collins joins Eric for "Layla," "Knock on Wood," and "You Don't Know Like I Know." Carl Perkins also joins the lineup for "Matchbox," "Blue Suede Shoes," and "Goodnight Irene."

Left: With Phil Collins at Guildford Civic Hall, October 20, 1985. (Stuart Pearsall)

21

Limehouse Television Studios, London

Eric takes part in a concert tribute to Carl Perkins. Eric plays on "Matchbox," "Mean Woman Blues," "That's Alright Now Mama," "Blue Moon of Kentucky," "Night Train," "Glad All Over," "Whole Lotta Shakin' Goin' On," "Blue Suede Shoes." Other guests included George Harrison, Ringo Starr, Earl Slick, Rosanne Cash, and

Dave Edmunds. The show is set for broadcast on New Year's Day 1986.

23

Halle Des Fetes, Lausanne, Switzerland

24

Hallenstadion, Zurich

27, 28

Theatro Tenda, Milan

29

Palasport, Turin

31

Palasport, Naples

NOVEMBER 1985

1

Palaeur, Rome

2

Palasport, Genova

4

Theatro Tenda, Bologna

5

Palasport, Florence

6

Palasport, Padova

On his return to England, Eric plays on a session for Paul Brady. Also *Edge of Darkness* is broadcast by the BBC. Eric's haunting music receives high praise.

DECEMBER 1985

3

Dingwalls, Camden, London

Eric joins Buddy Guy and Junior Wells halfway through their set for a wonderful and unexpected jam. Eric had been watching from the side of the stage and had not even brought a guitar. Buddy let him use his ESP guitar.

9

Theatro Tenda, Milan

Eric jams with Sting on "Down So Long" and on the encore.

12

The Dickens Pub, Southend, Essex

Eric joins Gary Brooker and friends for a small charity concert, calling themselves The Pier Head Restoration Band.

13

The Parrot Pub, Forest Green, Surrey

The Pier Head Restoration Band performs again.

19, 22

Hammersmith Odeon, London

Eric plays with Dire Straits for their Christmas season concerts. He plays on "Two Young Lovers," "Cocaine," "Solid Rock," and "Further on Up the Road."

23

Village Hall, Dunsfold, Surrey

Eric joins Gary Brooker for a special concert which also features Mick Fleetwood and Albert Lee.

FEBRUARY 1986

Eric plays on a session for Canadian acoustic guitar virtuoso Leona Boyd.

23

Jams with Rolling Stones at 100 Club in London's Oxford Street alongside Pete Townshend and Jeff Beck.

25

Presents Rolling Stones with their Lifetime Achievement Award at the Grammy Awards, live from the Roof Gardens Club in Kensington and relayed by satellite to Los Angeles.

1986

MARCH 1986

Paul Brady releases his *Back to the Centre* album. Eric plays on "Deep in Your Heart."

APRIL 1986
6

Eric appears in sketch at Comedy Aid and sings in the chorus during "Feed the World" with Bob Geldof and Midge Ure.

8

Short interview on Radio One.

Most of April and May is spent recording *August* at Sunset Sound in Los Angeles.

Tracks recorded include "Miss You," "Tearing Us Apart," "Lady From Verona," "Behind the Mask," "Run," "Bad Influence," "Walk Away," "Hung Up on Your Love," "Take a Chance," "Hold On," "Walking the White Line," "Holy Mother," and "Grand Illusion."

The sessions are produced by Phil Collins who also plays

drums. Tina Turner guests on "Tearing Us Apart" and "Hold On." The rest of the band are Greg Phillinganes on keyboards and backing vocals and Nathan East on bass.

JUNE 1986
20

Eric appears at the Prince's Trust tenth birthday party concert at Wembley Arena alongside Midge Ure, Mark

King, Phil Collins, Mark Knopfler, Elton John, Rod Stewart, Mick Jagger, David Bowie, Tina Turner, Sting, Howard Jones, Joan Armatrading, Paul McCartney, Bryan Adams, Francis Rossi, Rick Parfitt, Paul Young, George Michael, and John Illsley.

The show is filmed and recorded for later release. Bowie and Jagger's version of

Right: With Lionel Richie at New York's Madison Square Garden. (Chuck Pulin/Starfile)

106

"Dancing in the Street" is the only song not released from this concert.

28

Rehearsals start for upcoming tour. Band now consists of Phil Collins on drums, Nathan East on bass, and Greg Phillinganes on keyboards.

JULY 1986

3

Isle Of Calf Festival, Oslo

4

Roskilde Festival, Copenhagen

9

Jazz Festival, Montreux
On the eve of his own performance Eric jams with Otis Rush alongside Luther Alison. Complete show broadcast on Swiss radio.

10

Jazz Festival, Montreux
Robert Cray jams with Eric on "Ramblin' on My Mind" and "Have You Ever Loved a Woman." The show is filmed and recorded.

12

Juan Les Pins Festival, Antibes

14, 15

NEC, Birmingham, England
Both shows are recorded; 15th is filmed. Robert Cray jams on "Further on Up the Road" on 15.
Basic set for the tour is "Crossroads," "White Room," "I Shot the Sheriff," "Wanna Make Love to You," "Run," "Miss You," "Same Old Blues," "Tearing Us Apart," "Holy Mother," "Behind the Mask," "Badge," "Let It Rain," "In the Air Tonight," "Cocaine," "Layla," "Sunshine of Your Love," and "Further on Up the Road."

17

Capital Radio, London, broadcasts Eric Clapton interview.

AUGUST 1986

11

Lionel Richie releases *Dancing on the Ceiling* LP. Eric plays on "Tonight Will Be Alright."

14

Eric jams with Prince at The Gardens nightclub, Kensington, on a few Al Green numbers.

Eric Clapton: Oh, that was great. He played "Can't Get Next to You," an old Al Green song, for about half an hour. Prince saw me and invited me up.

15

Charity cricket match at Finchley Cricket Club. Eric jams with Chicken Shack during the post-match party.

16

Eric and band film video for "Tearing Us Apart" at Ronnie Scott's Club in London's Soho. An invitation only audience is treated to several versions of this track and various instrumental jams including Prince's "1999."

21

Eric attends Bob Geldof's stag party at Groucho's in Soho.

27, 28

Records with Bob Dylan at London's Townhouse Studios in Shepherds Bush, with Ronnie Wood on bass and Henry Spinetti on drums. They record three takes of "The Usual," one of "Song With No Name," seven of "Had a Dream About You," three of "Five and Dimer," and one of "To Fall in Love."

29

Leona Boyd releases her *Persona* LP. Eric plays on "Labyrinth."

SEPTEMBER 1986

Eric records two tracks for the soundtrack of *Color Of Money*: "It's in the Way That You Use

1986

AUGUST

UK Duck Records WX71 925
476-1
US Duck Records 25476
Released November 1986

Side One:
1. It's in the Way That You
   Use It
2. Run
3. Tearing Us Apart
4. Bad Influence
5. Walk Away
6. Hung Up on Your Love

Side Two:
7. Take a Chance
8. Hold On
9. Miss You
10. Holy Mother
11. Behind the Mask

Above: (Vinnie Zuffante/
Starfile)

Far right, above: With
Roomful of Blues guitarist
Ronnie Earl. (Steve
Weitzman/Starfile)

Far right, below: With Keith
Richards at the Ritz Club,
New York, November 1986.
(Gene Shaw/Starfile)

It" which appears on the *August* LP and "It's My Life Baby" on which he is backed by the Big Town Playboys but which remains unreleased.

OCTOBER 1986
16

Fox Theater, St. Louis
    Eric plays at Chuck Berry's two sixtieth birthday concerts, singing and playing on "Wee Wee Hours." The concerts are filmed and recorded for later release.

Eric Clapton: Chuck appeared and he sat down next to me on a couch and said, "Hi, I'm Chuck Berry, you're Eric Clapton. Nice to meet you." Then he said, "Hang on a second" and shouted, "Bring the camera in." Then he

started to interview me about him!

27

Madison Square Garden, New York
    Joins Lionel Richie for "Tonight Will Be Alright."

29

Eric plays "Miss You," "It's in the Way That You Use It" and "I Shot the Sheriff" with house band on *Nightlife.*

NOVEMBER 1986
8

Eric joins Robert Cray at London's Mean Fiddler for "Smoking Gun," "Playing in the Dirt," "The Last Time," "Bad Influence," and "Phone Booth." The final song was

released as a free flexi-disc with the May issue of *Guitar Player* magazine.

Eric Clapton: It's a lovely band to play with. It's easy to slot in with someone like that because all the songs he writes are so natural and still loosely within a blues framework.

20, 21

The Metro, Boston. Opening of short club tour.

23, 24

The Ritz, New York
    Keith Richards joins Eric for "Cocaine" and "Layla" on 23.
    August LP released on 24.
    Bob Geldof releases his first solo album *Deep in the Heart*

1986/ 1987

of Nowhere. Eric plays on "Love Like a Rocket," "August Was a Heavy Month," "The Beat of the Night," and "Good Boys in the Wrong."

DECEMBER 1986

8–16

Records *Lethal Weapon* soundtrack at Townhouse Studios in London's Shepherds Bush.

23

Village Hall, Dunsford, Surrey. Plays with Gary Brooker in charity show.

25

Eric's Birmingham NEC show from July 15 is broadcast on British TV.

JANUARY 1987

The year starts with a British and European tour.

3, 4

Apollo, Manchester

5

"Behind the Mask" single released.

6, 7, 8

Royal Albert Hall, London
  Sting and Steve Winwood

join Eric for "Money for Nothing" and "Sunshine of Your Love" on 8.

10, 11, 12

Royal Albert Hall, London
  Phil Collins joins Eric for the last two shows on 11 and 12. All three shows are recorded but remain unreleased.

16

Ahoy Halle, Rotterdam

17

Forest National, Brussels

18

Le Zenith, Paris

20

Westfalenhalle, Dortmund, West Germany

21

Sporthalle, Hamburg

22

Festhalle, Frankfurt

23

Olympic Halle, Munich

26

Palatrussardi, Milan

29

Palaeur, Rome

30

Palasport, Florence
  The band for this tour comprised Mark Knopfler on guitar, Greg Phillinganes on keyboards, Nathan East on bass, and Steve Ferrone on drums. Mark played on all British dates as well as Brussels and Paris.
  The set was "Crossroads," "White Room," "I Shot the Sheriff," "Hung Up on Your Love," "Wonderful Tonight," "Miss You," "Same Old Blues," "Tearing Us Apart," "Holy Mother," "Badge," "Let It Rain," "Cocaine," "Layla," "Money for Nothing," and "Sunshine of Your Love."

FEBRUARY 1987

9

Eric receives BPI Award at Grosvenor House Hotel in London. The event is broadcast live on BBC1.

14

Bob Geldof and Eric perform

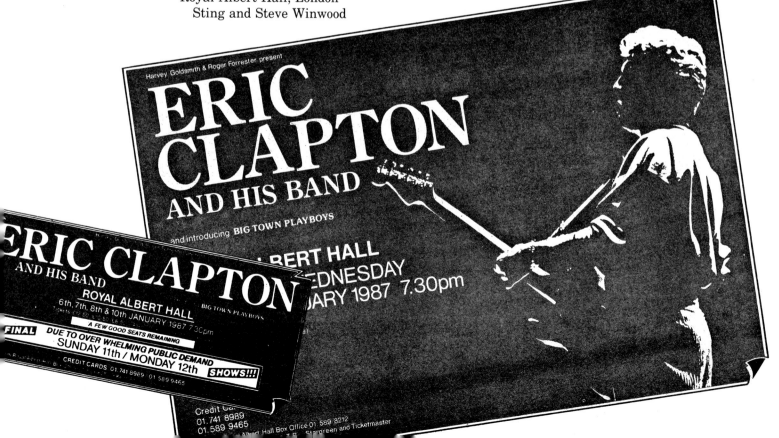

"Love Like a Rocket" on *Saturday Superstore*.

15, 16
Eric records three tracks with Jack Bruce, two of which are eventually released on *Willpower*.

19
Eric performs "Behind the Mask" on *Top of the Pops*.

MARCH 1987
2
Tina Turner releases "What You See Is What You Get" as a 12-inch single. Eric is credited as playing guitar.

23
"It's In the Way That You Use It" single released.

25
Attends Elton John's fortieth birthday party.

27
Eric plays charity gig at Cranleigh Golf Club in

Surrey. Numbers played include "Tulsa Time," "Behind The Mask," "Walkin' the Dog," "Route 66," "Cross-roads," "Lay Down Sally," "Black Magic Woman," "The Bear," "Alberta, Alberta," "Tearing Us Apart," "Knock on Wood," "Ramblin' on My Mind," "Red Dress," "Boogie," "Walkin' on Sunset," "Sunshine of Your Love," "Baby's Gone and Left Me," "Cocaine," and "Further on Up the Road."

APRIL 1987
11
Coliseum, Oakland, Cal. Start of U.S. tour.

13
Pacific Amphitheater, Costa Mesa

14
The Forum, Los Angeles

15
Ebony Showcase Theater, Los Angeles

1987

Right: With Robert Cray at New York's Madison Square Garden, 1987. (David Seelig/Starfile)

Below: (Gene Shaw/Starfile)

B. B. King special filmed here with Eric, Phil Collins, Chaka Khan, Gladys Knight, Paul Butterfield, Dr. John, Stevie Ray Vaughn, Albert King, Billy Ocean, and Etta James.

16
McNichols Arena, Denver

18
Civic Center, St Paul

19
Rosemont Horizon, Chicago
   After the show Eric, Phil Collins, and Robert Cray head down to the Limelight Club for a seventy-minute jam with Buddy Guy.

21
Market Square Arena, Indianapolis

22
Joe Louis Arena, Detroit

23
Richfield Coliseum, Cleveland

25
Capitol Center, Largo, Md.

26
Civic Center, Providence. This show is recorded but remains unreleased.

27
Madison Square Garden, New

York. This show is recorded but remains unreleased.
   The band for this U.S. tour comprised Phil Collins on drums, Greg Phillinganes on keyboards, and Nathan East on bass. The set consisted of "Crossroads," "White Room," "I Shot the Sheriff," "Hung Up on Your Love," "Wonderful Tonight," "Miss You," "Same Old Blues," "Tearing Us Apart," "Holy Mother," "Badge," "Let It Rain," "Cocaine," "Layla," "Further on Up the Road," and "Sunshine Of Your Love."
   As Robert Cray was the support artist for the tour he ended up jamming most nights on "Further on Up the Road."

MAY 1987
6
Eric joins Lionel Richie at Wembley Arena for "Tonight Will Be Alright" and "Brickhouse."

JUNE 1987
1, 2, 3, 4
Rehearsals at Brixton Academy for the upcoming Prince's Trust concerts.

5, 6
Wembley Arena, London
   Prince's Trust shows where

At the Prince's Trust concert, Wembley Arena, 1987. Eric on stage with, among others, George Harrison, Ringo Starr, and Jeff Lynne. (Vinnie Zuffante/Starfile)

Eric performed alongside Mark King, Midge Ure, Bryan Adams, Phil Collins, Ben E. King, Spandau Ballet, George Harrison, and Ringo Starr.

The highlight is an emotional version of "While My Guitar Gently Weeps" which features some great interplay between George and Eric.

The show on 6 is filmed and recorded for later release.

8

"Tearing Us Apart" single released.

John Astley releases his *Everyone Loves the Pilot* album. Eric plays on "Jane's Getting Serious."

18

Eric joins Tina Turner at Wembley for "Tearing Us Apart." The show is recorded and later broadcast on Radio One in England and released on album.

JULY 1987

4

Eric plays at Island Records' twenty-fifth birthday party at Pinewood Studios, performing "I Shot the Sheriff" with the Island All Stars. He later jams with Andy Summers, John Martyn, and Ringo Starr.

11

Star of six-part Radio One series on Eric called *Behind the Mask—The Story of Eric Clapton.*

AUGUST 1987

10

Prince's Trust concert released on album.

14

Eric plays in charity cricket match at Finchley Cricket Club and in the evening performs a ninety-minute set with Stan Webb's Chicken Shack. Numbers performed include "The Thrill Is Gone," "I'd Rather Go Blind," "Sweet Sixteen," "Further on Up the Road," "Every Day I Have the Blues," and "Cocaine."

SEPTEMBER 1987

4

Eric jams with Roomful of Blues at the Lone Star Café in New York. The same afternoon he'd filmed the *After Midnight* promo advertisement for a beer company at the club.

Eric Clapton: **Fantastic band. Ronnie Earl is a great player. They played their whole set then I got up and jammed with them. Phenomenal!**

14

Cream of Eric Clapton released.

OCTOBER 1987

6

Eric and Buddy Guy perform at Ronnie Scott's Club in Soho. Their set is filmed for inclusion on a *South Bank Show* TV special.

Eric Clapton: **They showed some of it on TV, late hours. I watched some of that and I was very disappointed with the sound mix because you can hardly hear Buddy.**

7

Bob Dylan's "The Usual" single, on which Eric guests, is released.

9

Buddy Guy plays the last of his two shows at Dingwalls in Camden Lock. Eric joins him for the final two-hour show. Among the highlights were "Stormy Monday," "Sweet Sixteen," "My Time After a While," and "The Things I Used to Do."

12

Sting releases his *Nothing Like the Sun* album. Eric plays acoustic guitar on "They Dance Alone."

19

Hearts Of Fire soundtrack released. Eric plays on "The Usual," "Night After Night," and "I Had a Dream About You."

23

Entertainment Centre, Sydney. Start of Australian and Japanese tour.

24

Entertainment Centre, Brisbane

27

Sports and Entertainment Centre, Melbourne

NOVEMBER 1987

2, 4, 5

Budokan, Tokyo

7

Nagoya Gym, Nagoya

9

Castle Hall, Osaka
   The band for these dates comprised Steve Ferrone on drums, Alan Clark on keyboards, and Nathan East on bass.
   George Harrison releases his *Cloud 9* LP. Eric plays on "Cloud 9," "That's What It Takes," "Devil's Radio," and "Wreck of the Hesperus."

DECEMBER 1987

6

South Bank Show TV documentary on Eric is broadcast in the UK. The program includes interviews with Eric, his mother, and grandmother, and also has rare footage from the unreleased *Rolling Hotel* film which documented his 1978 European tour.

Far left: (David Seelig/ Starfile)

Far left, inset: Eric shelters from the rain with, among others, Ian Botham and Bill Wyman. (Petra Zeig/Starfile)

Left: With Buddy Guy at Ronnie Scotts Club, London. (Marc Roberty)

Left, bottom: (Marc Roberty)

THE CREAM OF ERIC CLAPTON

UK Polydor ECTV1
No US release
Released September 1987

Side One:
1. Layla
2. Badge
3. I Feel Free
4. Sunshine of Your Love
5. Strange Brew
6. White Room
7. Cocaine
8. I Shot the Sheriff

Side Two:
9. Behind the Mask
10. Forever Man
11. Lay Down Sally
12. Knockin' on Heaven's Door
13. Wonderful Tonight
14. Let It Grow
15. Promises
16. I've Got a Rock'n'Roll Heart

1987/ 1988

CROSSROADS

UK Polydor 835 261-1
US Polygram 835261-1
Released April 1988

Record One Side One:
1. Boom Boom
2. Honey in Your Hips
3. Baby What's Wrong
4. I Wish You Would
5. A Certain Girl
6. Good Morning Little Schoolgirl
7. I Ain't Got You
8. For Your Love
9. Got to Hurry

Side Two:
10. Lonely Years
11. Bernard Jenkins
12. Hideaway
13. All Your Love
14. Ramblin' on My Mind
15. Have You Ever Loved a Woman

Record Two Side One:
16. Wrapping Paper
17. I Feel Free
18. Spoonful
19. Lawdy Mama
20. Strange Brew
21. Sunshine of Your Love
22. Tales of Brave Ulysses
23. Steppin' Out

Side Two:
24. Anyone for Tennis
25. White Room
26. Crossroads
27. Badge
28. Presence of the Lord
29. Can't Find My Way Home
30. Sleeping in the Ground

Record Three Side One:
31. Comin' Home
32. Blues Power
33. After Midnight
34. Let It Rain

19

Joins Gary Brooker, Henry Spinetti, and Andy Fairweather Low at Dunsfold Village Hall.

JANUARY 1988
22, 23

NEC, Birmingham. Start of UK tour.

Band comprised Steve Ferrone on drums, Nathan East on bass, Alan Clark on

keyboards, Ray Cooper on percussion, Mark Knopfler on guitar, and Katie Kissoon and Tessa Niles on backing vocals.

25, 26, 27, 29, 30, 31

Royal Albert Hall, London

FEBRUARY 1988
2, 3, 4

Royal Albert Hall, London

7

Civic Hall, Guildford. Elton John and Phil Collins join the band for various songs.

The set for this tour was "Crossroads," "White Room," "I Shot the Sheriff," "Wonderful Tonight," "Run," "Same Old Blues," "Tearing Us Apart," "Holy Mother," "Badge," "Let It Rain," "Cocaine," "Layla," "Behind the Mask," "Sunshine of Your Love," "Money for Nothing," and "Further on Up the Road."

8

Eric attends the BPI awards at London's Royal Albert Hall where The Who performs.

MARCH 1988
25

Eric records "The Robbery" at Townhouse Studios in London

for the soundtrack of *Buster*.

Eric Clapton: I just played some guitar. It was part of the score for the robbery scene which is quite early on in the film.

31

Tina Turner releases her *Live in Europe* double album. Eric plays on "Tearing Us Apart."

APRIL 1988
18

Crossroads retrospective released, containing many unreleased gems.

23, 24, 27, 28, 29

Eric records the soundtrack to *Homeboy* at Townhouse Studios in London's Shepherds Bush.

MAY 1988
7, 8, 14, 15, 21

Eric records the soundtrack to *Peace in Our Time* at Townhouse Studios.

30, 31

Rehearsals with Dire Straits at Brixton Academy.

JUNE 1988

1, 2, 3
Rehearsals with Dire Straits at Brixton Academy.

4
Rehearsals for Prince's Trust.

5, 6
Royal Albert Hall, London
Eric plays at these two Prince's Trust shows with Steve Ferrone on drums, Nathan East on bass, Mark Knopfler on guitar, Elton John on keyboards, Phil Collins on drums, and Katie Kissoon and Tessa Niles on backing vocals.

The set comprised "Behind the Mask," "Cocaine," "Money for Nothing," "I Don't Wanna Go on With You Like That," and "Layla." The concert concluded with all the evening's performers, including Phil Collins, Joe Cocker, Peter Gabriel, Howard Jones, the Bee Gees, Midge Ure, Wet Wet Wet, and T'Pau, joining in on "With a Little Help From My Friends."

7
Rehearsals with Dire Straits at Brixton Academy.

8, 9
Eric plays with Dire Straits at two warm-up shows at London's Hammersmith Odeon.

11
Eric joins Dire Straits at the *Free Nelson Mandela* concert at Wembley Stadium which is televised worldwide.

15–25
Eric records with Davina McCall.

23
This year's Prince's Trust show broadcast on TV.

35. Tell the Truth
36. Roll It Over
Side Two:
37. Layla
38. Mean Old World
39. Key to the Highway
40. Crossroads
Record Four Side One:
41. Got to Get Better in a Little While
42. Evil
43. One More Chance
44. Mean Old Frisco
45. Snake Lake Blues
Side Two:
46. Let It Grow
47. Ain't That Lovin' You
48. Motherless Children
49. I Shot the Sheriff
50. Better Make It Through Today
Record Five Side One:
51. The Sky Is Crying
52. I Found a Love
53. (When Things Go Wrong) It Hurts Me Too
54. Whatcha Gonna Do
55. Knockin' on Heaven's Door
56. Someone Like You
Side Two:
57. Hello Old Friend
58. Sign Language
59. Further on Up the Road
60. Lay Down Sally
61. Wonderful Tonight
Record Six Side One:
62. Cocaine
63. Promises
64. If I Don't Be There by Morning
65. Double Trouble
66. I Can't Stand It
67. The Shape You're In
Side Two:
68. Heaven Is One Step Away
69. She's Waiting
70. Too Bad
71. Miss You
72. Wanna Make Love to You
73. After Midnight

1988

Right: With Phil Collins, Rich Wills, and Mike Rutherford, Wintershall, July 1988. (Marc Roberty)

Below: (Marc Roberty)

JULY 1988

2

Charity show at Wintershall, Surrey, with Gary Brooker on keyboards and vocals, Phil Collins on drums and vocals, Andy Fairweather Low on guitar and vocals, Howard Jones on keyboards, Mike Rutherford on guitar, Henry Spinetti on drums, Jody Linscott on percussion, Rick Wills on bass, Frank Mead and Mel Collins on saxes, and Vicky and Sam Brown on backing vocals.

Among the songs in their two-and-a-half-hour set were "You Can't Hurry Love," "Abacab," "Wide Eyed and Legless," "No One Is to Blame," "Behind the Mask," "It's in the Way That You Use It," "Cocaine," and "Whiter Shade Of Pale."

4

"After Midnight" single released.

AUGUST 1988

Buckwheat Zydeco releases his *Taking It Home* LP. Eric plays on "Why Does Love Got to Be So Sad."

Eric Clapton: **He wasn't there when I did it. That came about through a mutual friend called Rob Fabroni who produced "No Reason to Cry." When Rob came to England earlier this year he brought the tape with him. I played on the thing . . . two takes.**

22–31

Rehearsals for upcoming North American tour in Dallas. Band comprises Alan Clark on keyboards, Jody Linscott on percussion, Mark Knopfler on guitar, Steve Ferrone on drums, Nathan East on bass, and Katie Kissoon and Tessa Niles on backing vocals.

SEPTEMBER 1988

1

Starplex Amphitheater, Dallas

2

Lakefront Arena, New Orleans

4

Civic Arena, Pittsburgh

6

Meadowlands Arena, East Rutherford, N.J.

7

The Spectrum, Philadelphia

8

Capitol Center, Largo, Md.

10

Civic Center, Hartford

11

Nassau Coliseum, Uniondale, N.Y.

13, 14

Great Woods, Mansfield, Mass.

16

Palace, Detroit

17

Alpine Valley, Milwaukee

19

Fiddler's Green, Denver

21

Shoreline Amphitheater, San Francisco

22

Arco Arena, Sacramento.

1988

23

Irvine Meadows Amphi-theater, Laguna Hills, Cal.

25

Hollywood Bowl, Los Angeles
Eric joins Elton John for "Saturday Night's Alright For Fighting."

26

Coliseum, Portland, Ore.

27

The Dome, Tacoma

28

PNE Coliseum, Vancouver

29

Pantages Theater, Los Angeles

Joins Little Feat for "Apolitical Blues."

30

Olympic Saddledome, Calgary, Alberta

OCTOBER 1988

1

Saskatchewan Place, Saskatoon, Saskatchewan

3

The Arena, Winnipeg, Manitoba

4

MET Center, Minneapolis

6

The Forum, Montreal

7

Maple Leaf Gardens, Toronto

8

Copps Coliseum, Hamilton, Ontario. Eric joined his support band Buckwheat Zydeco for "Why Does Love Got to Be So Sad."

The set throughout the U.S. and Canadian tour consisted of "Crossroads," "White Room," "I Shot the Sheriff," "Lay Down Sally," "Wonderful Tonight," "Tearing Us Apart," "After Midnight," "Can't Find My Way Home," "Motherless Children," "Same Old Blues," "Cocaine," "Layla," "Money for Nothing," and "Sunshine of Your Love."

10

Gail Anne Dorsey releases *The Corporate World* LP. Eric plays on "Wasted County."

11

Eric jams with Jack Bruce at New York's Bottom Line Club on "Spoonful" and "Sunshine of Your Love."

26–29

Rehearsals in Tokyo for Japanese tour.

31

Rainbow Hall, Nagoya

NOVEMBER 1988

2

The Dome, Tokyo
This show is filmed for subsequent broadcast on Japanese TV and radio.

4

Budokan, Tokyo
Sting joins Eric's band for "Money for Nothing."

5

The Stadium, Osaka
The band for Japan comprised Mark Knopfler on

guitar, Elton John on keyboards and vocals, Steve Ferrone on drums, Ray Cooper on percussion, Nathan East on bass, Alan Clark on keyboards, and Katie Kissoon and Tessa Niles on backing vocals.

The set consisted of "Crossroads," "White Room," "I Shot the Sheriff," "Lay Down Sally," "Wonderful Tonight," "Tearing Us Apart," "Can't Find My Way Home,"

"After Midnight," "Money for Nothing," "Candle in the Wind," "I Guess That's Why They Call It the Blues," "I Don't Wanna Go on With You Like That," "I'm Still Standing," "Daniel," "Cocaine," "Layla," "Solid Rock," "Saturday Night's Alright for Fighting," and "Sunshine of Your Love."

November also saw the release of *One Moment in Time* LP. Eric plays on The Bunbury's "Fight" alongside the Bee Gees on backing vocals, Laurence Cottle on bass, Duncan Makay on keyboards, and David English and Ian Botham on additional vocals.

28

Hard Rock Café, London
   Eric plays with Jeff Beck,

backed by Mitch Mitchell on drums and Noel Redding on bass, following a charity auction for the Celia Hammond Trust.

DECEMBER 1988

Jim Capaldi releases *Some Come Running* LP. Eric plays on "You Are the One" and "Oh Lord Why Lord," which also features George Harrison.

Eric Clapton: I played on two tracks. I played on more but I think two tracks are going to be used. It's a very good sounding record.

23

Dunsfold Village Hall, Surrey
   Eric plays with Gary Brooker, Andy Fairweather Low, Henry Spinetti, and Frank Mead.

Top, left to right: Mick Jones, Gene Cornish, Carole King, Eric, and Nathan East at New York's China Club, December 1988. (Dominick Conde/ Starfile)

Far left: Mark Knopfler. (Bob Gruen/Starfile)

1989

Also Eric appears on the *Wogan* show on TV on 25.

The set for the above U.K. dates was "Crossroads," "White Room," "I Shot the Sheriff," "Bell Bottom Blues," "After Midnight," "Wonderful Tonight," "Can't Find My

JANUARY 1989

10

Eric jams with Womack and Womack at Dingwalls in Camden Lock.

16

Sheffield City Hall. Start of UK tour.

The band consists of Phil Collins on drums, Nathan East on bass, and Greg Phillinganes on keyboards.

17

City Hall, Newcastle-on-Tyne

18

Playhouse, Edinburgh

20, 21, 22, 24, 25, 26, 28, 29, 30

Royal Albert Hall, London

Way Home," "Forever Man," "Same Old Blues," "Knockin' on Heaven's Door," "Easy Lover," "Tearing Us Apart," "Cocaine," "Layla," "Behind the Mask," and "Sunshine of Your Love."

FEBRUARY 1989

1, 2, 3

Royal Albert Hall, London

For the final six shows at the Albert Hall, Eric's band comprised Mark Knopfler on guitar, Steve Ferrone on drums, Nathan East on bass, Greg Phillinganes and Alan Clark on keyboards, Ray Cooper on percussion, and

1989

Katie Kissoon and Tessa Niles on backing vocals.

The set for these shows consisted of "Crossroads," "White Room," "I Shot the Sheriff," "Bell Bottom Blues," "Lay Down Sally," "Wonderful Tonight," "Wanna Make Love to You," "After Midnight," "Can't Find My Way Home," "Forever Man," "Same Old Blues," "Tearing Us Apart," "Cocaine," "Layla," "Solid Rock" (Feb 1, 2, and 3 only), "Behind the Mask," and "Sunshine of Your Love."

7

Eric records title music for the James Bond film *License To Kill* which remains unreleased due to legal problems.

MARCH 1989

Eric spends most of March and April at New York's Power Station and Skyline studios for the recording of *Journeyman* and *Lethal Weapon Two*. Tracks recorded include "No Alibis," "Old Love," "Hound Dog," "Before You Accuse Me," "Pretending," "Breaking Point," "Higher Power," "Hard

Top: With Ozzie Osbourne and Grace Jones. (Bob Gruen/Starfile)

Center: With Bill Wyman. (Pictorial Press)

Bottom: With Carl Perkins at New York's Bottom Line. (Chuck Pulin/Starfile)

Times," "Lead Me On," "Something About You," "Running on Faith" (two versions—one with electric guitar solo and one with dobro), "Murdoch's Men," "Anything for Your Love," "Run So Far," "Forever," and "Don't Turn Your Back."

APRIL 1989
3

Carole King releases her *City Streets* album. Eric plays on "City Streets" and "Ain't That the Way."

MAY 1989

Eric is back in New York for final overdubs and mixing of *Journeyman.*

9

Eric jams with Carl Perkins at New York's Bottom Line Club, and plays on "Mean Woman Blues," "Matchbox," "Roll Over Beethoven," "Maybelline," "Whole Lotta Shakin'," "Hound Dog," "Blue Suede Shoes," and "Goin' Down the Road Feeling Bad."

31

Eric attends the Elvis Awards ceremony at the Armory in New York and jams on an all-star finale of "I Hear You Knockin'" alongside Keith Richards, Jeff Healey, Tina Turner, Clarence Clemons, Vernon Reid, Dave Edmunds, and others.

Eric receives an Elvis Award for best guitarist, presented to him by Keith Richards.

JUNE 1989
5
Eric attends the reception following Bill Wyman's marriage to Mandy Smith along with various members of the Rolling Stones.

JULY 1989
1
Eric plays with Band Du Lac at a charity concert at Wintershall, Surrey.

The band consists of Gary Brooker on keyboards and vocals, Dave Bronze on bass,

Henry Spinetti and Phil Collins on drums, Frank Mead and Mel Collins on saxes, Sam and Vicki Brown on vocals, Andy Fairweather Low and Mike Rutherford on guitars, and Steve Winwood on keyboards.

The two-and-a-half-hour set includes "Pick Up the Pieces," "Ain't That Peculiar," "Can I Get a Witness," "Freedom Overspill," "Lead Me to the Water," "All I Need Is a Miracle," "Old Love," "Stop in the Name of Love," "You Don't Know Like I Know," "Respect," "Throwing It All Away," "A Bridge Across the River," "Lay Down Sally,"

"Souvenir of London," "Roll With It," "STOP," "Loco in Acapulco," "Gin House," "Cocaine," "Whiter Shade of Pale," "You Can't Hurry Love," "Night and Day," and "Gimme Some Lovin'."

6, 7
Statenhal, The Hague
Start of European, Middle Eastern, and African tour. Band consists of Steve Ferrone on drums, Nathan East on bass, Phil Palmer on guitar, Alan Clark on keyboards, Ray Cooper on percussion, and Katie Kissoon and Tessa Niles on backing vocals.

9, 10
Hallenstadion, Zurich

13
Sultan's Pool, Jerusalem

14
Zemach Amphitheatre, Sea Of Galilee, Israel

15, 17
Caesarea Amphitheatre, Caesarea, Palestine

22
Somhlolo National Stadium, Swaziland

25, 26
Conference Centre, Harare, Zimbabwe

28
Boipuso Hall, Gaborone, Botswana

30
Machava National Stadium, Maputo, Mozambique

This amazing concert was attended by 102,000 people who paid £1.00 a head. All proceeds were given to a local housing project. The concert was filmed.

Top: (C. Basiliano)

Inset: (John Peek)

Center: With Keith Richards at the Elvis Awards. (Bob Gruen/Starfile)

Bottom: (C. Basiliano)

1989

Right: With the Rolling Stones at Shea Stadium, October 1989. (Joel Levy/Starfile)

JOURNEYMAN

UK Duck Records WX322 926 074-1
US Duck Records 26074
Released November 1989

Side One:
1. Pretending
2. Anything for Your Love
3. Bad Love
4. Running on Faith
5. Hard Times
6. Hound Dog
Side Two:
7. No Alibis
8. Run So Far
9. Old Love
10. Breaking Point
11. Lead Me On
12. Before You Accuse Me

The set for this tour was "Crossroads," "White Room," "I Shot the Sheriff," "Bell Bottom Blues," "Lay Down Sally," "Wonderful Tonight," "I Wanna Make Love to You," "After Midnight," "Can't Find My Way Home," "Forever Man," "Same Old Blues," "Tearing Us Apart," "Cocaine," "Layla," "Badge," and "Sunshine of Your Love."

SEPTEMBER 1989
18

Stephen Bishop releases his *Bowling in Paris* LP. Eric plays on "Hall Light" which dates back to the *Behind the Sun* sessions.

28

Da Campo Boario, Rome
    Joins Zucchero Sugar Fornaciari for a version of "Wonderful World." Other guests at this concert include Clarence Clemons, Paul Young, and Dee Dee Bridgewater. The whole concert is shown on Italian TV.

OCTOBER 1989
7

Eric joins Elton John at Madison Square Garden in New York for "Rocket Man."

10

Eric joins the Rolling Stones at New York's Shea Stadium for "Little Red Rooster."

Eric Clapton: **The song I played was "Little Red Rooster" and I remember being taught how to play it by Howlin' Wolf himself 'cause we did an album together in London [*The London Howlin' Wolf Sessions*] and it was quite a hairy experience. He came over and got hold of my wrist and said, "You move your hand up HERE!"**

19

Eric joins the Rolling Stones at the Los Angeles Coliseum for "Little Red Rooster."

20, 21

Eric films the video for *Pretending* in Los Angeles.

25

Eric records a TV special with David Sanborn at New York's Rockefeller Center. They perform two takes of "Hard Times," "Old Love," and "Before You Accuse Me."

28

Eric and Pete Townshend are interviewed together on Sue Lawley's *Saturday Matters*. They perform a great acoustic version of Muddy Waters's "Standin' Around Cryin'."

NOVEMBER 1989
6

Journeyman released.

Eric Clapton: **I think it changed a little bit in the making. Pretty early on into the sessions we found that the material we were looking for would end up being like rock 'n' roll material. When we did "Hard Times," I said, "This is the kind of album I want to make" and Russ Tuitleman said, "Well, let's do that . . . definitely." Given the** fact that he made that smash hit album for Steve Winwood, I wanted to give him his head too. We agreed to postpone a blues album until our next project.

13

Polygram UK releases a special Collector's CD box set of *461 Ocean Boulevard, Timepieces,* and *Slowhand* along with a booklet.

17

Eric Clapton/David Sanborn TV special broadcast in U.S.

18

Royal Albert Hall, London

Eric plays "Edge of Darkness" with the Organic Symphony Orchestra conducted by Michael Kamen. Eric is introduced by George Harrison and is backed by Andy Newmark on drums and Ray Cooper on percussion. The event is in aid of Parents for Safe Food.

With George Harrison and Jeff Lynne, Eric joins Dame Edna Everage for the chorus of "Why Do We Love Australia."

The show also featured Wayne Eaglin and members of the Royal Ballet, Pamela Stephenson, and Billy

Connolly. The entire performance is filmed.

20

Phil Collins releases *But Seriously* album. Eric plays on "I Wish It Would Rain" and appears in the video for this song.

26

Eric attends Tina Turner's fiftieth birthday party celebrations at The Reform Club in London's St. James.

DECEMBER 1989
8, 9

Eric records *Communion* film soundtrack at Townhouse Studios, London.

Top: (Marc Roberty)

Center: With George Harrison at JFK Airport, New York. (Mike Wherman/ Starfile)

Left: With Jack Bruce, Bottom Line Club. (Michael Pawlyk/Starfile)

1989/ 1990

19
Convention Center, Atlantic City
  Eric joins the Rolling Stones for "Little Red Rooster" and "Boogie Chillin'" also featuring John Lee Hooker. The whole concert is broadcast live on pay-per-view TV.

23
Eric joins Gary Brooker's No Stiletto Shoes band for a special Christmas show at Chiddingford Ex-Serviceman's Club.

JANUARY 1990
14, 15, 16
NEC, Birmingham. Start of UK tour.
  These three shows were performed by the Four Piece Band (Eric, Steve Ferrone on drums, Nathan East on bass, and Greg Phillinganes on keyboards). The set comprised "Pretending," "I Shot the Sheriff," "Running on Faith," "Breaking Point," "Can't Find My Way Home," "Bad Love," "Lay Down Sally," "Hard Times," "Before You Accuse Me," "No Alibis," "Old Love," "Tearing Us Apart," "Wonderful Tonight," "Cocaine," "Layla," "Crossroads," and "Sunshine of Your Love."

17
BBC Theatre, Shepherds Bush, London
  Eric and band perform "Bad Love" on the *Wogan* TV show.

18, 19, 20, 22, 23, 24
Royal Albert Hall, London
  Six further shows by the Four Piece Band with a set comprising "Pretending," "Running on Faith,"

"Breaking Point," "I Shot the Sheriff," "White Room," "Can't Find My Way Home," "Bad Love," "Lay Down Sally," "Before You Accuse Me," "No Alibis," "Old Love," "Tearing Us Apart," "Wonderful Tonight," "Cocaine," "Layla," "Crossroads," and "Sunshine of Your Love."
  "Same Old Blues" was added to the program on 22. On 24 Phil Collins joined the

HARVEY GOLDSMITH BY ARRANGEMENT WITH ROGER FORRESTER PRESENTS

ERIC CLAPTON

RECORD BREAKING 18 NIGHTS

THE ROYAL ALBERT HALL

JAN 18, 19, 20, 22, 23, 24, 26, 27, 28, 30, 31, FEB 1
WITH HIS BAND

FEB 3, 4, 5
AN EVENING OF THE BLUES WITH SPECIAL GUEST

FEB 8, 9, 10
AN EVENING WITH
THE NATIONAL PHILHARMONIC ORCHESTRA
WITH MICHAEL KAMEN

TICKETS: £17.50, £15.00

ROYAL ALBERT HALL
STALLS
DOOR 4 HARVEY GOLDSMITH & ROGER FORRESTER PRES
ROW   G9   ERIC CLAPTON - A BLUES EVENING
SEAT 13   PLUS SUPPORT
092289
          SUNDAY   FEB. 04/90 AT 7:30 PM
PRICE   EVENING
17.50   DOORS OPEN 45 MINUTES BEFORE PERFORMANCE
1-ZZ
3-050508   PROMOTER   ZZ
          TO BE RETAINED SEE REVERSE FOR CONDITIONS OF SALE

Top: (Bob Gruen/Starfile)

Center and bottom: (Joel Levy/Starfile)

band for an encore of "Knockin' on Heaven's Door." The show on 24 was filmed and recorded.

26, 27, 28, 30, 31

Royal Albert Hall, London
Eric leads a thirteen-piece band for these shows: Phil Palmer on guitar, Nathan East on bass, Greg Phillinganes and Alan Clark on keyboards, Steve Ferrone on drums, Ray Cooper on percussion, Katie Kissoon and Tessa Niles on backing vocals, and Ronnie Cuber, Randy Brecker, Louis Marini, and Alan Rubin on horns.

The set comprised "Pretending," "Running on Faith," "Breaking Point," "I Shot the Sheriff," "White Room," "Can't Find My Way

130

Home," "Bad Love," "Lay Down Sally," "Before You Accuse Me," "Old Love," "No Alibis," "Tearing Us Apart," "Wonderful Tonight," "Cocaine," "Layla," "Crossroads," and "Sunshine of Your Love."

FEBRUARY 1990

1

Royal Albert Hall, London
Performance as above, which was filmed and recorded.

3

Royal Albert Hall, London
The first of the "Blues Nights" on which Eric headed a band comprising Robert Cray on guitar and vocals, Buddy Guy on guitar and vocals, Johnnie Johnson on piano, Jamie Oldaker on drums, and Robert Cousins on bass. The concert was divided into three sections, Eric leading the first before handing over the show to Robert Cray and Buddy Guy.

Eric's set comprised "Key to the Highway," "Worried Life Blues," "All Your Love," "Have You Ever Loved a Woman," and a medley of "Standin' Around Cryin'" and "Long Distance Call"; with Robert Cray leading, the band performed "Going Down Slow," "You Belong to Me," "Cry for Me," "Howling for My Baby," and "Same Thing"; and with Buddy Guy leading,

the band performed "Money (That's What I Want)," "Five Long Years," "Everything's Gonna Be Alright," "Something on Your Mind," "My Time After a While," "Sweet Home Chicago," "Hoochie Coochie Man," and "Wee Wee Baby."

The whole concert was broadcast live on BBC Radio One FM.

4

Royal Albert Hall, London
The second "Blues Night" with the band as above and a

set comprising "Key to the Highway," "Worried Life Blues," "Watch Yourself," "Have You Ever Loved a Woman," "Johnnie's Boogie," "Standin' Around Cryin'"/ "Long Distance Call," "Going Down Slow," "You Belong to Me," "Cry for Me," "Howling for My Baby," "Same Thing," "Money (That's What I Want)," "Five Long Years," "Something on Your Mind," "Everything's Gonna Be Alright," "Sweet Home Chicago," "My Time After a While."

1990

5

Royal Albert Hall, London

The third "Blues Night" with the band as above and "Wee Wee Baby" added to the set list. This show was filmed and recorded.

8, 9, 10

Royal Albert Hall, London

For these "Orchestral" shows Eric led an eight-piece band accompanied by the National Philharmonic Orchestra conducted by Michael Kamen. The band was the same as January 26 less the horn section. The set comprised "Crossroads," "Bell Bottom Blues," "Lay Down Sally," "Holy Mother," "I Shot the Sheriff," "Hard Times," "Can't Find My Way Home," "Edge of Darkness," "Old Love," "Wonderful Tonight," "White Room," "Concerto for Electric Guitar and Orchestra," "Layla," and "Sunshine of Your Love."

The show on 9 was filmed and recorded while the show on 10 was broadcast on Radio One FM.

Eric Clapton: I'm very grandiose, so I decided that this year's project had to be a really mammoth production. I've always been susceptible to classical music, and I thought it would be nice to have a concerto not just for a guitar but for *my* guitar.

14

Icehall, Helsinki

16

The Globe, Stockholm

17

Skedsmo Hall, Oslo

19

KB Hall, Copenhagen

20

Sporthalle, Hamburg

Rock Steady broadcasts part of Eric's "Blues Night" from February 5.

22

Forest National, Brussels

23

Grugahalle, Essen, West Germany

Ray Cooper injured his hand at this show and was unable to continue with the tour.

24

Statenhal, The Hague

26, 27

Palatrussardi, Milan

MARCH 1990

1

Olympic Halle, Munich

3, 4

Zenith, Paris

5

Festhalle, Frankfurt

The set for the European tour comprised "Pretending," "No Alibis," "Running on Faith," "I Shot the Sheriff," "White Room," "Can't Find My Way Home," "Bad Love," "Before You Accuse Me," "Old Love," "Tearing Us Apart," "Wonderful Tonight," "Cocaine," "Layla," "Crossroads," and "Sunshine Of Your Love."

24

Eric appears on *Saturday Night Live* in New York performing "No Alibis," "Pretending," and "Wonderful Tonight" with his band. After the cameras stopped rolling Eric jammed with the Saturday Night band, performing "Born Under a Bad Sign" and "Hideaway."

28

Omni, Atlanta. Start of American tour. The band is the same as for the European dates, and the set normally

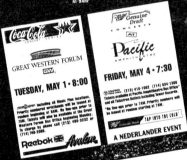

ROGER FORRESTER PRESENTS

AN EVENING WITH
ERIC CLAPTON AND HIS BAND

BOTH SHOWS
ON SALE TODAY
AT 9AM!

Coca-Cola CONCERT SERIES

GREAT WESTERN FORUM
GW

TUESDAY, MAY 1 • 8:00

Including all Music Plus locations.
Priority numbered wristbands will be issued at
random beginning at 9AM. No one can arrive at
7AM. Tickets will also be available at the Great
Western Forum Box Office beginning Monday.
To charge by phone call (213) 480-3232 or
(714) 740-2000.

Reebok **Avalon**

Miller Genuine Draft
CONCERTS AT
Pacific AMPHITHEATRE

FRIDAY, MAY 4 • 7:30

(213) 410-1062 (714) 634-1300
Tickets available at Pacific Amphitheatre Box Office
and all Ticketron Outlets including Tower Records.
*No one can arrive at 7AM. Priority numbers will
be issued at random starting at 7AM.

TAP INTO THE COLD

A NEDERLANDER EVENT

THE CONCERT COMPANY
MAMA CONCERTS & LIPPMANN + RAU

präsentiert von: **Frankfurter Rundschau**   Samstags mit der **ROCK RUNDSCHAU**

ERIC CLAPTON
and his BAND
special guest: Zucchero
Vorverkaufsbeginn MORGEN, SA. 18. November
5. März '90 · Frankfurt - Festhalle

KARTENSERVICE AN DER FESTHALLE
MESSE-FRANKFURT
Tel. 069 / 74 06 44

Sandrock
Hauptwache Passage
Tel. 069 - 20111/N

KARL HASS
Schillerstraße 11
6100 Multi2
Tel. 06131 - 228729

sowie bei
allen bek.
VVK Vorver-
kaufsstellen

ROYAL ALBERT HALL

STALLS	9 HARVEY GOLDSMITH & ROGER FORRESTER PRE
DOOR	K5
ROW	ERIC CLAPTON AND HIS BAND
SEAT	120

PLUS SUPPORT

TUESDAY   JAN. 23/90 AT 7:30

EVENING
DOORS OPEN 45 MINUTES BEFORE PERFOR

094099

PRICE
17.50
1-22
4-052193

PROMOTER   ZZ

TO BE RETAINED SEE REVERSE FOR CONDITIONS OF SALE

comprises "Pretending," "Before You Accuse Me," "Running on Faith," "I Shot the Sheriff," "White Room," "Can't Find My Way Home," "Bad Love," "Lay Down Sally," "No Alibi," "Old Love," "Tearing Us Apart," "Wonderful Tonight," "Cocaine," "Layla," "Crossroads," and "Sunshine Of Your Love."

30

Coliseum, Charlotte, S.C.

31

Dean Smith Center, Chapel Hill, N.C.

APRIL 1990

2

Madison Square Garden, New York
  Daryl Hall joins Eric for "No Alibis."

3

Meadowlands Arena, East Rutherford, N.J.

4

The Spectrum, Philadelphia

6

Nassau Coliseum, Uniondale, N.Y.

7

Carrier Dome, Syracuse

9, 10

Centrum, Worcester, Mass.

12, 13

Civic Center, Hartford

15

Palace of Auburn Hill, Detroit
  Stevie Ray Vaughan jams on "Before You Accuse Me" and "After Midnight."

16

Riverfront Coliseum, Cincinnati

17

Coliseum, Richfield, Minn.

19

Market Square Arena, Indianapolis

20

Hilton Coliseum, Ames, Ohio

21

The Arena, St. Louis

23

Lakefront Arena, New Orleans

24

The Summit, Houston

25

Reunion Arena, Dallas

27

McNichols Arena, Denver

29

Tingley Coliseum, Albuquerque

30

ASU Pavilion, Phoenix

MAY 1990

1

The Forum, Los Angeles
  George Harrison joins Eric for "Crossroads" and "Sunshine of Your Love."

3

Sports Arena, San Diego

4

Pacific Amphitheater, Costa Mesa, Cal.

5

Shoreline Amphitheater, San Francisco

JUNE 1990

5

The Armory, New York
  Eric rehearses with his band and Buddy Guy for next night's show. They play many blues and generally have fun.

6

The Armory, New York
  Eric plays at the 1990 Elvis Awards. He performs "Before You Accuse Me" with his band and is then presented with the Living Legend Award by Buddy Guy. Eric and band plus Buddy Guy, Dave Stewart, Richie Sambora, Neil Schon, Lou Reed, Bo Diddley, and Stephen Tyler then play "Sweet Home Chicago."

30

Nordoff-Robins Charity Concert, Knebworth, Hertfordshire.

Opposite page, far left, top: (Zoran Veselinovic/Retna)

Far left, center: (Pictorial Press)

Far left, below: With Elton John. (LFI)

Left, top: (LFI)

Left, center: (LFI)

Left, below: (Joel Levy/Starfile)

Overleaf: (Philip Ollersenshaw/Starfile)

Eric and his band play "Pretending," "Before You Accuse Me," "Old Love," and "Tearing Us Apart." They are then joined by Mark Knopfler for "Solid Rock," "I Think I Love You Too Much," and "Money for Nothing." Elton John then also joins in the fun for "Sacrifice," "Sad Songs," and "Saturday Night's Alright for Fighting." They encore with an extended "Sunshine of Your Love."

The whole concert is broadcast live on the radio. Part of the show is also released on video.

JULY 1990

Eric and his band return to America for the second part of their tour.

21, 22

The Arena, Miami
Eric and band rehearse at this venue.

23

The Arena, Miami

25

The Arena, Orlando

27

Suncoast Dome, St. Petersburg

28

Lakewood Amphitheater, Atlanta

30

Starwood Amphitheater, Nashville

31

Mid-South Coliseum, Memphis

AUGUST 1990

2

The Coliseum, Greensboro

3, 4

Capitol Center, Washington

6, 7

Meadowlands Arena, East Rutherford, N.J.

9, 10, 11

Great Woods, Mansfield, Mass.

13

Performing Arts Arena, Saratoga, N.Y.

14, 15

The Spectrum, Philadelphia

17, 18

Nassau Coliseum, Uniondale, N.Y.

21

Blossom Music Theater, Cleveland

22

Pine Knob Pavilion, Detroit

23

Riverbend Music Theater, Cincinnati

25

Alpine Valley Music Theater, East Troy
Eric is joined by Jeff Healey on "Crossroads" and "Sunshine of Your Love."

26

Alpine Valley Music Theater, East Troy
Eric is joined by Buddy Guy, Stevie Ray Vaughan, Jimmie Vaughan, and Robert Cray for "Sweet Home Chicago." Sadly this was to be Stevie Ray Vaughan's last show as the helicopter taking him and Eric's party crashed, leaving no survivors.

It was decided to finish the tour although it was extremely difficult for everyone concerned.

Eric Clapton: **There is a scene in the movie** *The Last Waltz* **where Robbie Robertson is explaining to Martin Scorsese that "the road is a goddamn impossible way of life" . . . I had never really agreed with that point of view until August when the road took the toll of four people who were very important to me . . . Colin Smythe, Nigel Browne, and Bobby Brooks were key members of our touring family and close personal friends; their contribution to the well being and smooth operation of our little unit is very sadly missed . . . Stevie Ray Vaughan was a great inspiration to me, truly one of the finest I ever heard. I miss them all.**

28

Sandstone Amphitheater, Kansas City, Kan.

29

The Arena, St. Louis

31

Thompson-Boling Arena, Knoxville

SEPTEMBER 1990

1

Oak Mountain Amphitheater, Birmingham

2

Coast Coliseum, Biloxi
Before heading off to South America for a tour, Eric went to New York for a guitar overdub on "Bad Love." This was done at Electric Lady Studios and used by Honda Cars for a Japanese television commercial.

The set for the upcoming world tour was as follows: "Pretending," "No Alibis," "Running on Faith," "I Shot the Sheriff," "White Room," "Can't Find My Way Home," "Bad Love," "Before You Accuse Me," "Old Love," "Badge," "Wonderful Tonight," "Cocaine," "Layla," "Crossroads," and "Sunshine of Your Love."

29

Estadio Nacional, Santiago, Chile

OCTOBER 1990

3

Estadio Centenario, Montevideo

5

Estadio River Plate, Buenos Aires

1990/ 1991

24 NIGHTS

Reprise Records 9 26420-2
Released November 1991

Disc One:
1. Badge
2. Running on Faith
3. White Room
4. Sunshine of Your Love
5. Watch Yourself
6. Have You Ever Loved a Woman
7. Worried Life Blues
8. Hoodoo Man

Disc Two:
1. Pretending
2. Bad Love
3. Old Love
4. Wonderful Tonight
5. Bell Bottom Blues
6. Hard Times
7. Edge of Darkness

7
Praca Da Apoteose, Rio De Janeiro

9
Ginasio Nilson Nelson, Brazilia

11
Ginasio Mineirinho, Belo Horizonte, Brazil

13
Orlando Scarpelli Stadium, Florianopolis, Brazil

16
Ginasio Gigantinho, Porto Alegre, Brazil

19, 20, 21
Olympia, Sao Paulo

October saw the release of a very special *Layla—20th Anniversary Edition* box set containing three CDs. As well as sounding better than ever, it also featured over two hours of previously unreleased material from the original sessions.

NOVEMBER 1990

Eric and His Band continue on their world tour.

7, 8
The Supertop, Auckland

10
Royal Theatre, Canberra

12, 13
Festival Theatre, Adelaide

15
National Tennis Centre, Melbourne

16, 17
Entertainment Centre, Sydney

19
Entertainment Centre, Brisbane

24
The Stadium, Singapore

26
Negara Stadium, Kuala Lumpur

29
The Coliseum, Hong Kong

DECEMBER 1990
4, 5, 6
Budokan, Tokyo

9
Olympic Pool, Tokyo

10
Rainbow Hall, Nagoya

11
Castle Hall, Osaka

13
The Arena, Yokohama

On his way home Eric goes via New York to record a couple of tracks with Lamont Dozier. He also receives the Billboard Music Award for "Top Album Rock Artist."

JANUARY 1991

Eric films the video for his new single "Bad Love" with Phil Collins. Phil was returning the favor as Eric had appeared in his video for "I Wish It Would Rain."

Eric and His Band play a couple of warm-up dates in Ireland before starting a mammoth season in London.

31
Dublin

FEBRUARY 1991
2
Dublin

Eric and his band continue the tradition of starting every new year by playing at London's Royal Albert Hall. This time, however, it was for a record-breaking twenty-four nights!

The set played by the four-piece band is as follows: "Pretending," "No Alibis," "Running on Faith," "I Shot the Sheriff," "White Room," "Can't Find My Way Home," "Bad Love," "Before You Accuse Me," "Old Love," "Badge," "Wonderful Tonight," "Cocaine," "Layla," "Crossroads," and "Sunshine of Your Love."

5, 6, 7, 9, 10, 11
Royal Albert Hall, London

Four-piece lineup with Eric, Phil Collins on drums, Nathan East on bass and vocals, and Greg Phillinganes on keyboards and vocals. Steve Ferrone replaced Phil Collins on 9, 10, 11.

13, 14, 15
Royal Albert Hall, London

Nine-piece lineup with the above four-piece and Phil Palmer on guitar, Ray Cooper on percussion, Chuck Leavell on keyboards and vocals, and Katie Kissoon and Tessa Niles on vocals.

The set played by the nine-piece is as follows: "Pretending," "No Alibis," "Running on Faith," "I Shot the Sheriff," "White Room," "Can't Find My Way Home," "Bad Love," "Before You Accuse Me," "Old Love," "Tearing Us Apart," "Wonderful Tonight," "Cocaine," "Layla," "Crossroads," and "Sunshine of Your Love."

17, 18, 19
Royal Albert Hall, London
Nine-piece lineup as above.

23, 24, 25, 27, 28
Royal Albert Hall, London

Blues band lineup with Eric, Jamie Oldaker on drums, Jimmie Vaughan on guitar, Jerry Portnoy on harmonica, Joey Spampinato on bass, Chuck Leavell on keyboards, Greg Phillinganes on keyboards, Johnnie Johnson on piano and vocals, Albert Collins on guitar and vocals, Robert Cray on guitar and vocals, and Buddy Guy on guitar and vocals.

The set played by the basic blues band is as follows: "Watch Yourself," "Hoodoo Man," "Hideaway," "Standin' Around Cryin'," "All Your Love," "Have You Ever Loved a Woman," "Long Distance Call," "It's My Life Baby," "Key to the Highway," "Wee

Wee Baby." Then with Johnnie Johnson, "Tanqueray," "Johnnie's Boogie." Then with Albert Collins, "Tired Man," "Mother-In-Law Blues," "Black Cat Bone." Then with Robert Cray, "I Feel So Glad," "Reconsider Baby," "Stranger Blues." Then with Buddy Guy, "Hoochie Coochie Man," "Little by Little," "My Time After a While," and an encore of "Sweet Home Chicago."

MARCH 1991
1

Royal Albert Hall, London
   Blues band lineup as above.
   The set played by the orchestra comprises: "Crossroads," "Bell Bottom Blues," "Holy Mother," "I Shot the Sheriff," "Hard Times," "Can't Find My Way Home," "Edge of Darkness," "Old Love," "Wonderful Tonight," "White Room," "Concerto for Electric Guitar," "Layla," and "Sunshine of Your Love."

3, 4, 5, 7, 8, 9

Royal Albert Hall, London
   Orchestra consists of nine-piece lineup plus the National Philharmonic Orchestra conducted by Michael Kamen.

Eric Clapton: **This year we set ourselves an almost impossible task of doing four different things. That meant you were rehearsing with four different kinds of musician and playing four different kinds of music. It was very taxing. We got through it but I think I bit off more than I could chew. I was extremely morose and tired and felt I'd conned myself into doing it. I don't think you can spread yourself that thin.**

All twenty-four nights were recorded and four of them filmed for a proposed double live album and video.
   Following his Albert Hall shows, Eric played on some sessions for Buddy Guy, Johnnie Johnson, and Richie Sambora.
   Eric was due for a well

deserved break with his family. Sadly fate struck another cruel blow when Eric's son, Connor, died in tragic circumstances in New York.

Eric Clapton: **My soul went dead to music. Music couldn't reach me. Immediately after his death I worked on very mundane things. I had to organize his funeral and look after the families. That kept me going. You remove yourself. You become like an official in a way. You become the person that everyone can go to with their suffering and it prevents you dealing with your own. That didn't happen until I went off on holiday with Roger [Forrester, Eric's manager] in May and I took a little gut-string guitar and I began playing. I found that a healing process. I would cry but I would play. And I started to write little songs which will probably be put out one day.**

Eric had abandoned mixing and selecting tracks for his new live album. The task was left to producer Russ Titelman.

Eric Clapton: **Russ Titelman selected the six best takes of everything for me to go through and choose. I wanted no part of anything, but I went into the studio just to keep my mind occupied and take it off the disaster. My part of the job didn't get done. I hated it because I thought, This was my life before. How can I relate to this? How can I get any enjoyment from it?**

AUGUST 1991

Eric plays on a session for Kate Bush.

Eric Clapton: **I had no idea what she wanted from me really, and I adore her music. In my fantasy head, I could see a way of doing it. I can see how it can be done in here, my head, but you give me the guitar and then lay down the track and tell me just do what I feel is right, then I've no idea. I really had to hand it**

over to her to tell me what to do really and I was surprised by the outcome. So it is really risky sometimes, it can be very frustrating.

Eric at the Royal Albert Hall, London. (Virginia Lohle/Starfile)

SEPTEMBER 1991
4

The Roxy, Los Angeles
   Eric joins Buddy Guy for a jam.
   Eric also starts work on the soundtrack for *Rush* at The Village Recorder in Los Angeles. Buddy Guy joined him for "Don't Know Which Way to Go." One of the other numbers that Eric recorded was the beautiful "Tears in Heaven" which became a huge worldwide hit for him.

29

The Palace, Hollywood
   Eric sits in with Nathan East's house band on the

1991/ 1992

UNPLUGGED

US Reprise Records 9 45024-2
Released August 1992
1. Signe
2. Before You Accuse Me
3. Hey, Hey
4. Tears in Heaven
5. Lonely Stranger
6. Nobody Knows you When You're Down and Out
7. Layla
8. Running on Faith
9. Walkin' Blues
10. Alberta
11. San Franciso Bay Blues
12. Malted Milk
13. Old Love
14. Rollin' and Tumblin'

JOSEPH ENTERTAINMENT BY ARRANGEMENT WITH ROGER FORRESTER PRESENT

AN EVENING WITH

ERIC CLAPTON

AND HIS BAND

WITH SPECIAL GUESTS
STEVIE RAY VAUGHAN & DOUBLE TROUBLE, THE ROBERT CRAY BAND FEATURING THE MEMPHIS HORNS

AUGUST 25 & 26 5:00PM

ALPINE VALLEY MUSIC THEATRE

TICKETS AVAILABLE AT ALL TICKETRON OUTLETS OR CHARGE BY PHONE (312) 899-SHOW OR (414) 271-2000.

Sunday Comics TV show. They play various instrumentals during the commercial breaks. The show ended with a superb version of "Further on Up the Road" and some great camera angles of Eric's finger work.

Eric also recorded some of the songs he had written during his healing period. These included, "Circus Left Town," "My Father's Eyes," "Lonely Stranger," and "Signe."

NOVEMBER 1991

Eric plays on a session for David Sanborn.

Most of November is spent rehearsing for George

Harrison's return to the live stage.

Eric Clapton: I was getting asked all over the world last year what George was up to. I felt it my duty to go and tell him. I don't think he realized how much interest there was. I said, Why don't you go and do some gigs? because I know it's the last thing he wants to hear. But I enjoy it so much that I'd like to share it with him. I don't think he's ever had the experience of playing for an audience with a great band. The Beatles played to ten-year-old kids who screamed their heads off. He stopped smoking, he's got himself into fighting fit shape. He's got my lighting, my sound, my band. We're going to Japan where

the world spotlight won't be on him and he probably won't get a bad review. It's a great opportunity.

DECEMBER 1991

Eric and his band back George Harrison for a Japanese tour. Andy Fairweather Low replaces Phil Palmer who has joined Dire Straits for "On Every Street" tour.

The set is as follows: "I Want to Tell You," "Old Brown Shoe," "Taxman," "Give Me Love," "If I Needed Someone," "Something," "Fish on the Sand," "Love Comes to Everyone," "What Is Life," "Dark Horse," "Piggies," "Pretending," "Old Love," "Badge," "Wonderful Tonight," "Got My Mind Set on You," "Cloud 9," "Here Comes the Sun," "My Sweet Lord," "All Those Years Ago," "Cheer Down," "Devil's Radio," "Isn't It a Pity," "While My Guitar Gently Weeps," and "Roll Over Beethoven." "Fish on the Sand" and "Love Comes to Everyone" are dropped after a few shows.

1
The Arena, Yokohama

2, 3
Castle Hall, Osaka

5
Kokusai-Tenjijo, Nagoya

6
Sun Plaza Hall, Hiroshima

9
Fukuoka Kokusai Center, Fukuoka

10, 11, 12
Castle Hall, Osaka

14, 15, 17
Tokyo Dome, Tokyo. George Harrison's son, Dhani, joins in for the encore on 17.

JANUARY 1992

Rush soundtrack is released.

Eric starts the new year with a television interview from his Chelsea home. He also plays a live version of "Tears in Heaven."

16

Bray Studios, Berkshire

Eric and his band play an amazing all acoustic concert which is filmed for MTV's *Unplugged* series as well as being recorded for a possible live album. The set list on the night ran as follows: "Signe," "Before You Accuse Me," "Hey Hey," "Tears in Heaven," "Circus Left Town," "Lonely Stranger," "Nobody Knows You When You're Down and Out," "Layla," "Signe (take 2)," "My Father's Eyes," "Running on Faith," "Walking Blues," "Alberta, Alberta," "San Francisco Bay Blues," "Malted Milk," "Signe (take 3)," "Tears in Heaven (take 2)," "My Father's Eyes (take 2)," "Rollin' and Tumblin," "Running on Faith (take 2)," "Walking Blues (take 2)," "San Francisco Bay Blues (take 2)," "Malted Milk (take 2)," "Worried Life Blues," and "Old Love."

Eric and band rehearse for a small UK tour.

FEBRUARY 1992

1

Brighton Centre, Brighton

The running order of the set differed slightly as the shows progressed. Initially the set was as follows: "Anything for Your Love," "Pretending," "I Shot the Sheriff," "Running on Faith," "My Father's Eyes," "She's Waiting," "Circus Left Town," "Tears in Heaven," "Signe," "Before You Accuse Me," "Old Love," "Badge," "Wonderful Tonight," "Tearing Us Apart," "Layla," "Crossroads," and "Sunshine of Your Love."

3, 4, 5

National Indoor Arena, Birmingham

7, 8

Sheffield Arena, Sheffield

12, 13, 14, 16. 17, 22, 23, 24 18,

Royal Albert Hall, London

By the time Eric and his band reach the Albert Hall, the set changed to: "White Room," "Pretending," "Anything for Your Love," "I Shot the Sheriff" (13 onward), "Running on Faith," "My Father's Eyes" (12 only), "She's Waiting," "Circus Left Town," "Tears in Heaven," "Signe," "Malted Milk" (17 onward), "Nobody Knows You When You're Down and Out" (17 onward), "Tearing Us Apart," "Before You Accuse Me," "Old Love," "Badge," "Wonderful Tonight," "Layla," "Crossroads," and "Sunshine of Your Love."

MARCH 1992

2, 3

S.E.C.C., Glasgow

27, 29

MTV broadcasts Eric's *Unplugged* in England.

APRIL 1992

Eric receives Lifetime Achievement Award at the Ivor Novello Awards held at London's Grosvenor House Hotel.

Eric Clapton: I love what I do because it's easy and seems to give people happiness.

Eric records soundtrack to *Lethal Weapon 3*.

17–23

Eric and his band rehearse at Las Colinas, Dallas, for upcoming U.S. tour. Gina Foster replaces Tessa Niles.

Set is taken from following: "White Room," "Pretending," "Anything for Your Love," "I Shot the Sheriff," "Running on Faith," "She's Waiting," "Circus Left Town," "Tears in Heaven," "Before You Accuse Me," "Old Love," "Badge,"

"Wonderful Tonight," "Layla," "Crossroads," and "Sunshine of Your Love."

25

Reunion Arena, Dallas

27

Lakefront Arena, New Orleans

28

Civic Center, Birmingham

29

The Pyramid, Memphis

MAY 1992

1

Thompson-Boling Arena, Knoxville

2

Coliseum, Charlotte, N.C.

4, 5

The Spectrum, Philadelphia

6

Civic Center, Hartford

8

Meadowlands Arena, East Rutherford, N.J.

10

Capitol Center, Washington

11

Dean Smith Center, Chapel Hill, N.C.

13, 14

Rosemont Horizon, Chicago

16

Bradley Center, Milwaukee

17

Target Center, Minneapolis

19

Market Square Arena, Indianapolis

20

Richfield Coliseum, Cleveland

21

Riverfront Coliseum, Cincinnati

1992/ 1993

23.
Omni, Atlanta

24
Suncoast Dome, St. Petersburg

25
The Arena, Miami
   At the end of the tour, Eric plays on a session for Ray Charles.

29
Eric attends the Rhythm of Life fashion show in aid of the Rainforest Foundation at London's Grosvenor House Hotel. The event is hosted by Sting and his wife, Trudie, who hope to raise £100,000 to help Indians defend their threatened Amazon forests.

JUNE 1992

Elton John releases *The One* album. Eric plays and sings on "Runaway Train" which is also on the soundtrack to *Lethal Weapon* 3.
   Eric and His Band prepare for a European tour. Some of the dates are double head-liners with Elton John.

Elton John: **I wanted someone who I really admired as a musician and have a great bill of music on the same day and Eric came to mind because I did a tour playing in Eric's band with Mark Knopfler in Japan, about three-and-a-half years ago, which was so much fun. I like him, we know each other quite well, we get on with each other and I think we are both at the peak of our powers at the moment, so it would be a good idea.**

14, 15
Rehearsals in Ghent, Belgium.

16
Flanders Expo, Ghent

18
Hippodrome De Vincennes, Paris (Elton John double bill)

19
Feyernoord Stadium, Rotterdam (Elton John double bill)

21
Olympic Riding Stadium, Munich

22
Waldbuehne, Berlin

23
Westfalenhalle, Dortmund, Germany

26, 27
Wembley Stadium, Wembley, England (Elton John double bill)
   Eric joins Elton John for "Runaway Train" on 26; Jimmie Rogers joins Eric for a jam on 27.

28
Wembley Stadium (Elton John double bill)
   Bonnie Raitt joins Eric on "Before You Accuse Me." No "Sunshine of Your Love," but Eric joins Elton for a version of "The Bitch Is Back" alongside Brian May, Curtis Stigers, and Bonnie Raitt.

JULY 1992

3
Pontaise Stadium, Lausanne, Switzerland (Elton John double bill)

4
St. Jakob Stadium, Basle, Switzerland (Elton John double bill)

6
Stadio Communale, Bologna, Italy (Elton John double bill)

10
Stadio Brianteo, Monza, Italy (Elton John double bill)

12
Montreux Jazz Festival, Montreux, Switzerland
   Show is recorded and "White Room" is filmed and used in TV documentary of the festival.
   Elton John/Eric Clapton release "Runaway Train" as a single.

23
Live video of Eric and Elton from Wembley Stadium playing "Runaway Train" shown on *Top of the Pops*.

AUGUST 1992

Unplugged released.
   Sting releases "It's Probably Me" as a single. Eric plays guitar on tunes from *Lethal Weapon 3* soundtrack album.

9, 10
Civic Arena, Pittsburgh
   Eric and his band rehearse at this venue before starting their U.S. tour.

11
Civic Arena, Pittsburgh

13
Meadowbrook Music Theater, Rochester.
   Eric joins Little Feat for "Mellow Down Easy" and "Apolitical Blues."

14
The Palace of Auburn Hills, Detroit

Eric with Robbie Robertson of The Band. (Dominick Conde)

17, 18

Great Woods, Mansfield, Mass.

19

Performing Arts Center Saratoga, N.Y.

21, 22

Shea Stadium, New York (Elton John double bill)

24

Poplar Creek Music Theater, Chicago

25

Riverport Amphitheater, St. Louis

29, 30

Dodger Stadium, Los Angeles (Elton John double bill)

SEPTEMBER 1992

3, 4

Shoreline Amphitheater, San Francisco

6

Tacoma Dome, Seattle

9

Pauley Pavilion, Los Angeles (MTV Awards)

Eric and band perform "Tears in Heaven" after he receives MTV award for Best Video.

After the tour Eric records a few demos with Steve Ferrone and Nathan East. One of the numbers is a new composition called "Hear Me Calling," a great blues song which will be given its first public hearing at the 1993 Royal Albert Hall shows.

21

The *Unplugged* version of "Layla" released as single.

OCTOBER 1992

1

NEC, Birmingham, England (charity show)

3

Sheffield Arena, Yorkshire, England (charity show)

16

Madison Square Garden, New York

Eric joins all-star cast for an amazing concert tribute to Bob Dylan who was celebrating his thirtieth anniversary in the industry. Eric plays "Love Minus Zero" and "Don't Think Twice," backed by the house band, G. E. Smith on guitar, Duck Dunn on bass, Jim Keltner on drums, and Steve Cropper on guitar. Eric later joined in the grand finale with the all-star band led by Bob Dylan, playing "My Back Pages" and "Knockin' on Heaven's Door." Eric's guitar work was particularly expressive and it was a real joy to see and hear Neil Young exchanging licks with him during these encores.

JANUARY 1993

Eric records some new songs with Robbie Robertson.

12

Plaza Hotel, Los Angeles

Cream re-forms for the Rock 'n' Roll Hall of Fame awards, playing "Sunshine of Your Love," "Crossroads," and "Born Under a Bad Sign." The show is filmed and recorded.

Jack Bruce: **Me, Ginger, and Eric are good friends now and the intervening time has made us a lot mellower. As far as Cream went, the animosity between us was a little exaggerated. We all met again at the induction ceremony and the old spirit was still there. I**

Eric Clapton with Bob Dylan at the all-star concert in October 1992 celebrating Dylan's thirty years as a recording superstar. (Chuck Pulin)

Eric with his six Grammys, Los Angeles, March 1993. (Jeffrey Mayer)

Eric and Al Green at the rehearsal for the ''Apollo Hall of Fame'' awards in New York City. (Chuck Pulin/Starfile)

guess it was a bit of a millstone round our necks but doing that Hall of Fame gig made me realise that people love it still. We are seriously looking at doing reunion dates, probably sooner rather than later. I know Eric's keen — maybe I've got to instigate it myself to make it happen.

FEBRUARY 1993

2

Eric is presented with the Royal Variety Club award for Outstanding Recording Artist of 1992.

Eric decides to perform exclusively blues for this year's Royal Albert Hall concerts.

Eric Clapton: I grew up from an early age listening to and absorbing this wonderful music and I remember being fascinated by the variety of forms it could take. I realized quite soon in my appreciation that it is not, as many people think, just a bunch of guys jamming on a twelve bar, it is in fact a very ordered and compact musical structure often requiring a great deal of discipline and economy in its performance . . . The songs I have chosen to play at the Albert Hall highlight the development of the blues from its early beginnings until now, and will include the works of Leroy Carr, Robert Johnson, Big Maceo, Big Bill Broonzy, Muddy Waters, Little Walter, Jimmie Rogers, Howlin' Wolf, Elmore James, Bobby Bland, Albert King, Freddy King, Buddy Guy, and maybe even myself . . . I should point out that my performance is not intended to be an academic presentation of the history of the blues, that would be no fun. I would rather you think of it as an invitation to join me on a journey back through the music that has given me so much inspiration and pleasure in my life.

The set consists of: "How Long," "Alabama Women," "Terraplane Blues," "From Four Until Late," "Kidman Blues," "County Jail Blues," "32-20," "Chicago Break-down," "Hey Hey," "Walkin' Blues," "Long Distance Call," "Blow Wind Blow," "Key to the Highway," "Tell Me Mama," "Juke," "Blues Leave Me Alone," "Going Away Baby," "Coming Home," "Meet Me in the Bottom," "Forty Four," "It's My Life," "Love Her With a Feeling," "Tore Down," "Born Under a Bad Sign," "Let Me Love You Baby," "Groaning the Blues," "Hear Me Calling," "Ain't Nobody's Business," "Sweet Home Chicago."

Most of the shows are recorded for possible later release. Jimmie Vaughan is the support and jams most nights on the encore, "Sweet Home Chicago."

20, 21, 22, 23

Royal Albert Hall, London
    On 20, Eric plays "Blues With a Feeling" and "Further on Up the Road." "All Your Love" was also played for the first few dates before being dropped in favor of longer guitar solos.

24

Eric flies out to Los Angeles to receive an amazing six Grammy Awards.

26, 27

Royal Albert Hall, London
    On 26, Buddy Guy jams on the encore "Sweet Home Chicago."

MARCH 1993

Ray Charles releases his *My World* album. Eric plays on "None of Us Are Free."

1, 2, 3

Royal Albert Hall, London

5, 6, 7

Royal Albert Hall, London
    Lou Ann Barton sings on the encore of "Sweet Home Chicago."